Start Your Own

MEDICAL CLAIMS BILLING SERVICE

Additional titles in *Entrepreneur's **Startup Series***

Start Your Own

Bed & Breakfast

Business on eBay

Business Support Service

Car Wash

Child Care Service

Cleaning Service

Clothing Store

Coin-Operated Laundry

Consulting

Crafts Business

e-Business

e-Learning Business

Event Planning Business

Executive Recruiting Service

Freight Brokerage Business

Gift Basket Service

*Growing and Selling Herbs
    and Herbal Products*

Home Inspection Service

Import/Export Business

Information Consultant Business

Law Practice

Lawn Care Business

Mail Order Business

Personal Concierge Service

Personal Training Business

Pet-Sitting Business

*Restaurant and Five Other
    Food Businesses*

Self-Publishing Business

Seminar Production Business

Specialty Travel & Tour Business

Staffing Service

Successful Retail Business

Vending Business

Wedding Consultant Business

Wholesale Distribution Business

Entrepreneur
MAGAZINE'S

startup

Start Your Own

2ND EDITION

MEDICAL CLAIMS BILLING SERVICE

Your Step-by-Step Guide to Success

Entrepreneur Press and Jennifer Dorsey

EP
Entrepreneur
Press

Editorial Director: Jere L. Calmes
Managing Editor: Marla Markman
Cover Design: Beth Hansen-Winter
Production and Composition: Alicen Armstrong Brown

This publication is designed to provide accurate and authoritative information in regard to the subject matter covered. It is sold with the understanding that the publisher is not engaged in rendering legal, accounting, or other professional services. If legal advice or other expert assistance is required, the services of a competent professional person should be sought.

Library of Congress Cataloging-in-Publication Data
Start your own medical claims billing service/by Entrepreneur Press and Jennifer
    Dorsey.—2nd ed.
        p.   cm.
    Rev. ed. of: Start your own medical claims billing service/Rob and Terry Adams.
        c2003.
    Includes bibliographical references and index.
    ISBN 1-59918-150-9 (alk. paper)
        1. Medical fees—Data processing—Handbooks, manuals, etc. 2. Health insurance claims—Data processing—Handbooks, manuals, etc. 3. New business enterprises—Handbooks, manuals, etc. 4. Medical offices—Management—Handbooks, manuals, etc. 5. Medicine—Practice—Finance—Handbooks, manuals, etc. I. Adams, Rob, 1950-Start your own medical claims billing service. II. Dorsey, Jennifer. III. Entrepreneur Press. IV. Title: Medical claims billing service.

R728.5.A297 2007
651.5'042610285—dc22   2007033135

Printed in Canada

12 11 10 09 08 07   10 9 8 7 6 5 4 3 2 1

Contents

Chapter 10

Blowing Your Own Horn 139

Chapter 11

More Pain Management: Controlling Your Finances 159

▲

Preface

You're holding this book in your hands, on your lap, or on your desk—probably dangerously near a spillable cup of coffee—because you're one of those people who like to live on the edge. You're contemplating starting your own business.

This is one of the most exhilarating things you can do for yourself and your family. It's also one of the scariest.

Owning your own business means you're the boss, the big wheel, the head cheese. You make the rules. You lay down the law. It also means you can't call in sick (especially

▲

when you are also the only employee), you can't let somebody else worry about making enough to cover payroll and expenses, and you can't defer that cranky client or intimidating IRS letter to a higher authority. You're it.

We're assuming you've picked up this particular book on starting and running a medical billing business for one or more of the following reasons:

- You have a background in the medical billing field.
- You have a medical background of another sort.
- You've watched every episode of *Dr. Kildare, Marcus Welby, M.D., St. Elsewhere or ER* (depending, of course, on your individual taste and age group) and feel that although brain surgery is a little out of your league, it would be glamorous and exciting to have some connection to the world of medicine.
- You have a background in bookkeeping and believe that billing is billing.
- You have no background or interest in any of the above but believe medical claims billing is a hot opportunity and are willing to take a chance.

Which did you choose? (Didn't know it was a test, did you?)

Well, you can relax because there is no wrong answer. Any of these responses is entirely correct so long as you realize that *they all involve a lot of learning and a lot of hard work*. They can also involve a heck of a lot of fun, as well as a tremendous amount of personal and professional satisfaction.

Our goal here is to tell you everything you need to know to:

- decide whether medical claims billing is the right business for you and then, assuming it is, to:
  - get your business started successfully;
  - keep your business running successfully; and
  - make friends and influence people. (That's actually part of Chapter 10, which is about advertising and public relations.)

We've attempted to make this book as user-friendly as possible. We've interviewed lots of people out there on the front lines of the industry to find out how the medical billing business really works and what makes it tick. And we've set aside lots of places for them to tell their own stories and give their own hard-won advice and suggestions, sort of a virtual round-table discussion group with you right in the thick of things. (For a listing of these successful business owners, see the Appendix.) We've broken our chapters into manageable sections on every aspect of start-up and operations (the running your business kind, not the brain surgery kind). And we've left some space for your creativity to soar.

So sit back—don't spill that coffee!—start reading and get ready to become a medical billing pro.

For Mickie

1

Prescription
for Success

This chapter explores the burgeoning field of medical billing, or medical claims processing, from passé paper claims to progressive—and profitable—computerized billing.

▲

Think of this chapter as an investigative report—like those TV news magazine shows but without the commercials. We will explore the phenomenal growth of the medical billing field and the secrets of America's health-care billing industry.

The Doctor's Key

A medical billing service is the doctor's key to getting paid. Despite the fact that the health-care industry is alive and well in America, most doctors and other health-care providers have no idea how to get themselves paid quickly and efficiently, if at all—either by insurers or by patients who are also waiting for that check to arrive in the mail. Private and government-administered insurance companies, HMOs, PPOs, and a host of other mysteriously initialed plans have conspired to make physician re-imbursements as elusive as the pot of gold at the end of the rainbow. Doctors, once the lords of the health-care world, are fast becoming the underdogs. Not to worry—the medical billing service is on hand to save the day. A billing expert can dramatically increase the doctor's immediate revenue.

Through the miracle of cyberspace, the biller electronically transmits insurance claims directly to the insurance company, or, in other words, into the company's check-generating computers.

Amazingly, however, while electronic claims processing is *the* method for getting providers paid, most providers are still stuck in the "Snail Mail" age. This makes electronic billing a thriving field with room for growth.

Not a Small World

With legions of providers and an ever-expanding patient pool, the health-care industry is flourishing. According to the U.S. Department of Health and Human Services Centers for Medicare and Medicaid, health spending will continue to grow by 6.9 percent per year through 2016. By then, health-care spending will total $4.1 trillion and account for 19.6 percent of the gross domestic product (GDP). Consider the historical hard numbers. Americans spent around $2 *trillion* for health care in 2005 alone, about $6,697 per person. So let there be no doubt: Health care is big business. And, like Jack's legendary beanstalk, its growth shows no signs of slowing. This makes it fertile ground for the medical billing entrepreneur.

As Rod Serling of *The Twilight Zone* might say, we offer for your consideration the following:

America's ranks are swelling. According to the Centers for Disease Control and Prevention and the National Center for Health Statistics, life expectancy is on the upswing while infant mortality is mercifully on the downhill run. End result: more Americans roaming around. And that means more people to request or require health-care services.

Especially since more and more of us are finding ourselves in the once-inconceivable category of Older Americans. Legions of baby boomers are now past the half-century mark. This means two things: a) gray and/or thinning hair will soon become the "in" thing; and b) according to the U.S. Census, 78.2 million boomers are jockeying for position with Medicare. The four million babies born every year are adding ranks to the younger generations who will, one day, be first in line for benefits.

> ## Fun Fact
> The U.S. Census Bureau has a POPClock Projection you can access through the internet (www.census.gov/cgi-bin/pop clock). This site updates the resident population daily by tallying births, deaths, and international immigrant arrivals.

So, in plain English, what does all this mean to someone planning to start a medical billing business? Income.

A plethora of older Americans means more health-care dollars spent at the doctor's office. (As more than one retiree is wont to say, "They ought to call it the Rust Age instead of the Golden Age.") From arthritis to arteriosclerosis to prostate problems, cardiac care and cataracts, it all adds up to more and more money spent on health care (currently around $2 trillion a year, if you'll recall). Which, in turn, means more and more Medicare and secondary insurance claims to be filed.

Bevies of babies also equal health-care dollars. Think ear infections, colic, colds, chronic diaper rash, and all the other ills junior humans are prey to and you will realize that the rash of babies translates to a steady stream of pediatric patients. Which, in turn, translates to a steady stream of insurance claims to be filed.

What's a Provider?

In the health-care world, a provider is not only a physician but anyone who provides health-care services. Ambulance services, biofeedback technicians, and social workers are included, along with the non-M.D. doctors we call dentists, chiropractors, optometrists, podiatrists, and psychologists. Doctors specializing in everything from pediatrics to geriatrics, neurology to urology, are also, of course, providers. Purveyors of durable medical equipment, such as walkers and wheelchairs, count. So do specialists in hearing aids and prosthetic limbs. And don't forget nursing homes and hospices. They are providers, as are pharmacies.

These not-so-fine distinctions are important to keep in mind because you can consider them all potential clients for your medical billing service.

What Are People Spending?

Type of Service	Annual Personal Expenditures*	Private Health Insurance*	Government*	Other*
Physician	$286.4	$136.7	$95.2	$8.4
Dentist	60.0	30.1	2.8	0.2
Home Health Care	32.4	7.6	16.9	0.1
Nursing Home Care	92.2	7.4	55.9	1.9

*All figures are in billions. Source: Health Care Financing Review

Preventive Maintenance

Americans in the age range between teething and losing teeth are also big spenders in the health-care arena. Preventive maintenance used to be something you performed on your car or boat. Now it applies to people.

Just about everybody is into health and fitness these days, which means cholesterol tests, blood sugar tests, weekend athlete injury repairs, liposuction, and psychological tune-ups. People weaned on new medical techniques as seen on television are far more apt to see a doctor for a real or perceived health problem than ever before. Which—again—equals more patients, more bills, and more insurance claims to be filed.

The Problem

However—and this is a biggie—the doctor has little hope of receiving any income from all this patient activity if he can't get reimbursement from the insurance companies.

In the precomputer world, the payment process was protracted but simple. After being treated, the patient gave his insurance form (with his portion completed, you hope) to the doctor's receptionist and walked away, secure in the knowledge that dear Dr. Whosit would fill out all the boxes, send it in, and sit back and wait to be paid.

Which was exactly what happened. After a period of up to three months or so, the insurance company, having leisurely processed the form, sent a check to Dr. Whosit. The doctor's receptionist entered the check into his accounts receivable and then billed the patient for the balance. And Dr. Whosit waited another month or more for that money to trickle in.

Sometime in the '80s, doctors decided this system was unfair and began insisting that patients pay for services rendered before leaving the office, send in their own insurance claims and let the insurer reimburse them.

Nice try. The tables turned in 1990 when congressional law made it mandatory for doctors to complete and submit their patients' Medicare forms. Providers' efforts to achieve timely payments had been foiled again. There is, however, a happy ending to this tale—for the doctor wise enough to employ a medical billing service.

Electronic Filing Beats Paper

Medicare gives priority to any claims submitted electronically. Claims received online are paid in 10 to 14 days, as opposed to paper claims, which are set on the back burner for at least 29 days. Most other insurers now follow this same tenet—electronic claims before paper. The results can be dramatic.

Smart Tip

Unless you're an economics major, statistics probably make your eyes cross. But you can use them to your advantage: to impress potential clients and to woo potential investors (money people love facts and figures).

Consider this example from a medical biller near Chicago: "[Previously, the client] would type out a CMS [claim form] and send it to Illinois Medicare. It would be weeks before she'd know anything," he says, describing the way one of his clients used to do claims processing. He took over her billing, shot it off to Medicare, and within four days had online confirmation that the claims had been paid.

He explains that a four-day turnaround is a little faster than usual, and that, while the doctor didn't have the check in her hand, Illinois Medicare's tracking software allowed him to show her that her claims had indeed already been processed.

Needless to say, she was impressed.

Software Magic

Electronic billing might seem like magic. Result-wise, it is. But like stage magic, which is all done with smoke and mirrors, there's a method behind it. It's all done with software.

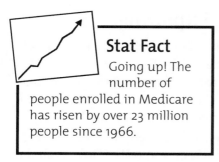

Stat Fact

Going up! The number of people enrolled in Medicare has risen by over 23 million people since 1966.

In precomputer days, the person in charge of filling out patients' insurance forms (usually a "front office" medical assistant as opposed to a "back office" assistant, who performs the nurse-type duties, such as drawing blood and giving injections) sat at her desk with a head-high stack of charts.

With the skill of an Egyptologist deciphering hieroglyphics, the biller worked through each chart, decoding the doctor's scrawl into the type of services or procedures performed and the diagnosis, then typing this information onto whichever form the patient had supplied. Next, she had the doctor sign each form, which was then stuffed into a corresponding envelope, stamped, and consigned to the U.S. mail. Then, of course, came the long wait for the form to reach the insurance company and be processed before the doctor could finally be reimbursed.

Phasing Out Paper

The CMS-1500 form (formerly the HCFA 1500) is still in use, but sparingly and only by a select group that must meet certain governmental requirements (see the CMS website for information on qualification). The form is used when a provider qualifies for a waiver from the Administrative Simplification Compliance Act (ASCA) requirement for electronic submission of claims. So what's wrong with paper? In a word, time. According to the CMS, paper claims providers submit to Medicare must be read with Optical Character Recognition (OCR), a scanning technology that allows hard copy data to be read by a computer and converted to a form that can be used as electronic data. In other words, OCR turns paper data into usable electronic data. The wording, columns, and tables your naked eye sees on the CMS-1500 form are printed in ink that is invisible to the OCR equipment, so only the usable fields can be seen and used. You must use the official CMS-1500 forms available from the U.S. Government Printing Office or authorized printer because they print with Flint OCR Red (J6983) ink. If you print the form on your own computer, your run-of-the-mill ink will show up to the OCR equipment, and it will be returned to you for resubmittal. The moral of the story is, if you are eligible to use paper, use the official forms. You can find Medicare CMS-1500 completion and coding instructions, as well as the print specifications in Chapter 26 of the Medicare Claims Processing Manual (Pub.100-04).

Skimming Along with Superbills

That was then. Now doctors who are electronic billing–savvy fill out a *superbill*, also called a *charge slip*, before the patient leaves the office. The superbill is divided into sections. One portion lists, in dazzling detail, the services and procedures commonly performed by the doctor. Another catalogs the symptoms and diagnoses the doctor usually treats. Each item on the list has a corresponding code number.

The doctor simply checks the box next to the service or procedure he's performed, makes another little tick next to the diagnosis or symptom, and voilà! There is all the information the medical biller needs. A superbill for a patient suffering from stomach flu, for example, would have a check next to 99212 (Established Patient Focused Straight Forward) for a routine, uncomplicated office visit and a check next to 558.9 (Gastroenteritis) for tummy virus, pizza-with-anchovies-and-clam-sauce-not-recommended.

The medical biller takes this streamlined superbill, enters the procedure and diagnosis codes into a claim form, called a CMS 1500, on his computer and then electronically sends it to the insurance company in the same way you might send an e-mail message. The insurer instantly receives the claim. No more delays waiting for mail delivery. No more lost time waiting for the claim to wend its way through knee-deep stacks of other paper claims. And no more painful paper cuts on your tongue from licking envelopes.

This is the Dick-and-Jane version of modern medical billing. There are many permutations and there can be many complications, which we will delve into later. (If you just can't wait, check out Chapter 3 now.) Really good medical billers learn all sorts of tips and tricks to make their work easier and to make the doctor's business—and therefore their own—more lucrative.

Counting Your Coconuts

Stat Fact
The percentage and the number of children (people under 18 years old) without health insurance increased between 2004 and 2005, from 10.8 percent to 11.2 percent and from 7.9 million to 8.3 million, respectively, says the U.S. Census Bureau.

What can you expect to make as a medical insurance biller? The sky's the limit, depending only on how serious you are and how willing you are to expand. Annual gross revenues for the industry range from $25,000 to $100,000. Some MIBs (that's medical insurance billers, not "Men in Black") are happy working part time at home, bringing in enough to supplement the family income. Others have launched thriving, full-time businesses that employ dozens of assistants.

Kim H., a medical biller in rural Virginia, runs her business in conjunction with a full-time career as a high school teacher. "Keep in mind," she says with a soft twang, "that I'm doing this part time, and with our area here being very small and economically disadvantaged, I had to set my limits." Still, she says, the part-time one-woman income she's pulling in is nothing to sneeze at.

Across the country, a San Diego MIB feels that her fledgling full-time business is off to a good start. At the other end of both the spectrum and the state, Walnut Creek, California, on MIB is well into her 13th year in business with a staff of 22, and is quite pleased with her income as well.

Stat Fact
According to the Census Bureau, there were 4.2 million Americans aged 85 plus tootling around the country at the time of the 2000 census. That represents increases over 1990 census figures of 35.4 percent in the 85- to 89-year-old category; 44.6 percent in the 90-94 category; and 34.7 percent in the 95 and over category!

However you choose to tailor your business—part time or full time, at home or in an outside office—the income potential is excellent. But almost everyone in this industry is quick to point out that medical billing is not an easy business.

"This is definitely not something that just anybody could do," explains Curt J., an MIB in Illinois. "Between the personal marketing skills and relating to professionals and doctors, and the learning curve on the code side and the computer side, it's been a challenge. [But] I enjoy a challenge."

One MIB in Denver has offered classes for people interested in starting a medical billing service. "Basically, [I taught] coding, terminology, how to deal with insurance companies, all of that stuff," she says. "And it was really an eye-opener to a lot of people. They just had no clue that to do it right and get and maintain clients you have to know what you are talking about."

Her classes experienced a lot of attrition. "I had probably about 50 percent who felt it was too much work," she explains. "They really wanted something where they could just pick up superbills, put them in their computer, and not worry about it again. And that just doesn't work."

Balance that with the words of an MIB in New Jersey who quit a ten-year career on the other side of the fence—working for a health insurer—to operate her homebased business. "I loved my job," she says. "I loved being on that side. But I would never go back to working for someone else, either."

One for All

The medical biller's most basic tool is the CMS 1500 (formerly the HCFA 1500). This daunting form is a detail-lover's dream, rife with boxes, bars, and spaces to be filled in, checked off, and tabulated, and is used to file all insurance claims. The CMS, as it is commonly referred to (though some still call it the HCFA), is the brainchild of the American Medical Association and is named for the Center for Medicare and Medicaid Services (CMS).

Before 1984, when the original HCFA 1500 was born, hundreds of different claim forms floated across the medical biller's desk: the American Medical Association's basic form and various versions of Medicare, Blue Cross, Blue Shield, Medicaid, and Civilian Health and Medical Program for the Uniformed Services (CHAMPUS) forms. In addition to these, most insurance companies had their own forms. The horrendous hodgepodge of blanks to be filled in was not only time-killing but conducive to error.

The American Medical Association (AMA) decided that enough was enough and created a task force to bring forth order from chaos. The result was the HCFA 1500, a single, standard form accepted by every insurer in the country.

In 1990, the HCFA went under the knife for further streamlining. The spaces where providers could write in explanations for out-of-the-ordinary fees were eliminated, lending the form the same impatient "I don't want to hear any excuses" tone you used to hear from your parents when you were in trouble. Now called the Center for Medicare and Medicaid Services, or CMS, the group is the main governing body for all things governmental as related to health care.

Prognosis: Success

So now that you have a nodding acquaintance with some of the many facets of this vital business (the formal introduction will come later), you're probably wondering what your chances of success are. After all, starting a business is a serious proposition, particularly when you have to put your hard-earned money where your CMS 1500 is.

Well, take heart. There's plenty of life in this business if you're willing and able. Perhaps even more importantly, you can make a go out of this profession no matter where you live, according to Tammy Harlan, president of Santiago SDS Inc., a medical billing business opportunity in LaPorte, Indiana. "We service 800 clients, and the biggest one is a $2.5 million operation in Nebraska," she says. "When I operated my own medical claims service, I worked out of Indiana, but I had clients as far away as California. Word of mouth helped me get new business, and I was willing to spend the money needed to get the appropriate business resources and training."

We'll talk more about those business resources later. But for now, just remember that your own ambition and motivation are just as important as upfront money when it comes to driving your success. As mentioned earlier, attention to detail and persistence are other necessary components for success in this people-driven field. Plus, there are numerous outside forces that can influence your success. For instance, if you live near a large metropolitan area, you'll have a larger pool of prospects to plumb, plus you'll be able to charge more per claim. Being internet savvy (or being willing to learn) also will help you increase your reach even further.

If you like to eat regularly, you might want to ease into your new profession. Realistically speaking, it could take several months before you land that first client. But whatever you do, Tammy says, you need to invest in all the tools you need to make it work, including business support and instruction.

"I know it's hard to spend money when you're just starting out, but it's an investment," Tammy says. "You might end up spending $8,000 to get started, but you could end up with a business for the rest of your life."

Crank-Up Costs

One of the Catch-22s of being in business for yourself is that you need money to make money—in other words, you need start-up funds. These costs are relatively small for a medical billing service. You can start out homebased, which means you don't need to worry about leasing office space. You don't need to purchase a lot of inventory, and you probably won't need employees. Your basic necessities are a computer (it's hard to do electronic filing without one), a printer, a modem, and a specialized software package. If you already have a computer, your biggest expense will be your software.

Many MIB newbies opt for a business opportunity package, purchasing not only the software but also the training to go with it. Different packages, even within the same company, have different costs. Some entrepreneurs go with strictly software because they're already billing-literate; others because the full biz op package doesn't fit into their budget.

The choice of which package to purchase is a personal one, approached by most MIBs with the same dedication and attention to personalities as you would attach to finding a mate. And rightly so. You are going to be wedded to your software package for a long time, and the business opportunity vendor you choose should fit your needs and your temperament like Adam and his rib.

We'll cover this in greater depth later in this book. For now, let's say that you can expect your start-up costs to run from about $5,000 to $20,000.

The Rock of Gibraltar

In addition to profits and start-up costs, two other important aspects to consider are risk and stability. You want a business that, like the Rock of Gibraltar, is here to stay. According to MIBs, there aren't any tremors rocking the structure of the industry. The risk factor is relatively low—so long as you are willing to work, and in most cases work hard, for that first client or two. "Doctors aren't just out there ready and waiting for you to walk through the office and save them," says the Illinois MIB. It can take time.

"Getting that first [client] is the toughest," explains the San Diego entrepreneur. "It's really tough, because if you don't have a client, then you have no basis, no credibility for [doctors] to rely on you. This is a big thing that they're giving up. A lot of doctors have a hard time giving up the financial end of things.

"Some people are looking for a get-rich-quick scheme. This is not the type of business to do that. You can be successful and make good money at this, but like any business, I believe, it takes time for the business to build, and it takes time to generate a positive influx of income."

Dollar Stretcher

Why not work at home? A medical billing service is a perfect candidate for a homebased business. The necessary equipment fits neatly into a spare room and, since clients don't need to visit your office, you don't have to spend start-up dollars on expensive furnishings, décor, or reception areas.

The Right Stuff

OK, so you've decided that running a medical billing service is potentially profitable. You're willing to invest not only the money but the time to learn the ropes and become established as a pro. What else should you consider? Personality.

Not everybody is cut out to be an MIB. This is not, for example, a career for the organizationally challenged. If you're one of those carefree folks who take a haphazard, devil-may-care approach to life, you don't want to be a medical biller. If your idea of filing is throwing papers in a stack behind your desk until the stack topples, you might

Traits of the Trade

Hey kids! Take this fun quiz and find out if you have what it takes to become an ace MIB.

1. *My idea of a fun evening is:*
   a. watching Casablanca on television for the 50th time
   b. snuggling up with a hot toddy and a book of advanced Sudoku
   c. barhopping with a guy named "Swinger Pete"

2. *Here's how I handle my daily mail:*
   a. Pick out the Publishers Clearing House and Overdue! Second Notice! envelopes and throw the rest in a drawer.
   b. Sort it by date received, date due, and action to be taken.
   c. Use it to start a fire in the barbecue pit for tonight's dinner.

3. *I consider myself to be a detail-oriented person.*
   a. True

4. *There is nothing wrong with Question 3.*
   a. True
   b. False
   c. Sorry, I wasn't paying attention.

5. *I would best describe my self-motivational abilities as follows:*
   a. What is self-motivation?
   b. I'm not happy unless I'm getting things accomplished.
   c. I'm able to get up in the morning.

Answers: If you chose B for each answer (and you noticed that there is no B answer for Question 3), then you passed with flying colors! You have what it takes to become an MIB. You are detail-oriented, self-motivated, and eager to learn.

look elsewhere for job inspiration. If you're an A-plus procrastinator who can't seem to return a phone call or pay a bill until it's overdue, think again about medical billing.

If, on the other hand, you're an efficient time manager, you excel at detail-oriented tasks, and your idea of heaven is getting things shipped out, shaped up, signed, sealed, and delivered, then this is the career for you.

Move Over, Miss Moneypenny

This doesn't mean that only supersecretary types like James Bonds' Miss Moneypenny need apply. MIBs come from all walks of life. The entrepreneurs interviewed for this book, for instance, come from a variety of careers: high school teacher, pastor who currently doesn't have a ministry, computer customer service engineer, registered nurse, and bookkeeper. Others made less radical career-style changes, having worked in the health-care, insurance, and medical billing professions before, but as employees rather than as the self-employed.

The tip here is that the first ones—the set that started from different career paths—have figured out how to make their backgrounds work for them in their new careers. They've taken the skills they've already acquired and applied them to the medical billing service.

For Kim H., the computer and business course teacher from Virginia, picking up electronic billing was a snap. So were the small-business aspects of running a medical billing service, which meant the only thing she needed to focus on was the actual medical coding.

"I knew a lot about the business part of it and the computer part of it," Kim explains, "but the insurance part I didn't know, so I had to learn that. It took me about two months to really grasp the insurance part. I got [the business opportunity package] in January 1996. By May, I had signed my first doctor, a psychiatrist. I guess about three months after that, I signed a urologist." Kim now has two more clients to keep her busy along with her full-time teaching career.

People Skills

Curt J., the pastor, transferred his people skills to his medical billing service, which he began in early 1997. "My personality is such that I can make a fairly good first impression," he says, describing his marketing approach. He had no background in sales, but Curt says that as a pastor, he knew how to get along with people. Part of his pastoral training was in working with people. "It's all personal skills but, in a sense, it's selling, too.

"The learning curve [for medical coding and billing] was much greater than I anticipated. It's not a simple business. I wanted to pick one that looked like it had potential for the future and could make money, but, on the other hand, I didn't want to pick one that just anybody could do," Curt says.

Mary V., the former customer service engineer, translated the people skills she'd learned working for IBM—as well as her knowledge of computers—into the medical billing business she started in 1993. "Basically, as a customer engineer," she says in a lively but no-nonsense tone, "all you did was problem-solve. And that's what this business is—problem-solving.

"Learning to work with people, I couldn't have gotten any better training. Personally, I think [IBM] is the best service company in the world, and they have the best training. So that was perfect for going into this. Whether it's medical billing or anything else, if you're dealing with a service-oriented company, you've got to know how to give service. And that's what this is."

One nurse-turned-MIB received her training in England. "When I came over here," she explains, "I tried to transfer my credits over, but at that point in time it was not possible. I had to go back and do some retraining, and I chose not to do that."

The career path she chose instead led, not quickly, but very directly, to the exact skills she would need to run her own highly successful medical billing business. She became an audiometrist, then a medical assistant at an ear, nose, and throat practice. "And within a year," Jan says, "I was administrator of that group." With more than 11 years of experience at that position, "I went into hematology-oncology and was an administrator for a large practice from '83 to '89, and then I started the billing service."

The other registered nurse spent almost 12 years on the post-op surgical floor. When an on-the-job injury permanently sidelined her career in scrubs, she parlayed her knowledge of the medical field into the medical billing service she started in 1997.

The former bookkeeper, Carol G., took her familiarity with all things billable and segued it into her own medical billing service. "I've worked for small businesses," she says, "and you work hard. You can only make so much per hour. It's nice to have a little more of what you're working for be on my end instead of working for someone else."

And isn't that one of the main reasons for starting your own business? The freedom to do things your own way, at your own speed, in your own home or office, is a powerful lure.

The Great Debate

As you can see, you don't have to have a medical background to become a top-notch MIB, but it helps. Among MIBs, however, a debate of sorts rages. Those with medical billing backgrounds insist that without that background, only fools rush in. Those who came into the business from other venues admit to the challenge of a major learning curve but are proof that with a great deal of preparation and hard work and the added bonus of support from a software or business opportunity vendor, it can be done.

The nurse whose background involves years of medical office administration is of the "no prior experience-no success" school. "It's the Johnny-come-latelies who don't do terribly well," she says sympathetically but firmly. "Maybe some lady who believes in starting a billing service, working on a PC in her home, and has had experience in billing, can probably do very, very well. If it's somebody who believes that it's just an easy thing to do, that person is in for some pretty rude awakenings. A lot of businesses that are in homes are not making it; their experience is not adequate to do what they're doing."

The Denver MIB works from her home rather than from offices in a commercial building, as her San Francisco Bay-area counterpart does, but she voices similar sentiments. Like her cross-country compadre, she started her business with an extensive background in medical billing and administration.

"I started probably 12–13 years ago, working in a physician's office as a receptionist," the Denver-based MIB says. "I became office manager, [then] I worked as a personnel trainer in the medical field. So I've always been behind the front desk. I never really did the billing until I moved out here to Denver and worked for a large billing service and got familiar with the insurances they use out here. And [then I] decided that I could do it on my own. I really liked that aspect of it.

The Self-Starter

Being a self-employed MIB, like everything else in life, has drawbacks along with the perks. A big one is that you have to be what is commonly referred to in help-wanted ads as a "self-starter." There's no one else around to tell you what to do or when to do it. If you want to run a medical billing service, you'd better make sure that your self-motivation gears are well-oiled.

"Even if I have my clients' billing done," says Carol G. from her home office in Missoula, Montana, "I'm making contacts or I'm looking at ideas, or if I hear of someone, I'm making that advertising contact."

You also need to keep in mind that all the responsibility for your business rests on your shoulders, however broad they may or may not be. "At times, you wish you could sit back and let somebody else fix the problems," the former bookkeeper explains. "The good and the bad stop right here."

But you don't feel bad about it, Carol's quick to add. "Even when I was working full time, when I would come to work [in the medical billing home office], it wasn't work; it was what I was enjoying doing. You have to discipline yourself to make it what you want with those things in mind."

Bright Idea

Ask a billing service to let you sit in on their operations for a few days. You can "audit" the service, observing what they do and how they do it. (You might want to pick a service outside your own area so you don't look like a competitor.) Or, why not volunteer to work for them for free for a few weeks? You get free experience and on-the-job training; they get free labor and a chance to strut their stuff.

"Since I had worked for physicians as a receptionist and a transcriptionist, I felt that I knew what went on in the office and could provide a good service rather than some of the billing services—some of the larger ones, anyway—that aren't really familiar with the inside workings of a physician's office. I felt that helped me a lot in kind of working up from ground zero."

She also thinks that this wealth of experience represents the dividing line between the successful medical billing services and those that face a struggle. "I taught some evening classes on how to bill for a time simply because I had a lot of phone calls," she explains. "People who wanted to [know] 'How did I get started in this business?' 'I'm thinking about doing this from home,' that kind of thing. One of the questions I always asked was 'What kind of experience do you have?' and most of the time what they would say was 'Well, I know computers.'

"And that's the big fallacy. I find it comes from software companies who are selling the billing software: 'We'll train you; you don't need any experience; all you have do is put the data in.'

"That's just unfair. That's unfair to people to spend money on software and think that they can just enter data. What I say to them at that point is, 'How are you going to speak to a physician and convince him that you can handle his money and that you can bring in money for him when you don't know what he does and you don't know his medical turf?'"

What exactly do you need to know? Why wouldn't a person be able to pop a diagnosis of X into the computer, and away they go?

"Well, they can enter it into the computer," the Denver MIB cheerfully concedes. But there is more. Much more. "It's not so much the diagnosis—well, it is the diagnosis, just as much as it is the procedure code. Say they have a diagnosis of depression. They put it in with just an office visit and send it out to the health-care company, and the health-care company sends back a denial saying 'We're not going to pay this. This is a mental disorder.'

Smart Tip

"If you're really going to succeed in it," Mary V. says of the MIB industry, "you're going to have to [be learning] almost every day." Be sure you're willing to make that commitment.

"What then? Does someone who does not have the knowledge know how to handle that? All of a sudden they're stuck. 'OK, I'm not going to get paid for this; I don't know why.'

"It's the wrong code. It's only going to get paid at 50 percent; they need to send it someplace else. They need to know what a mental disorder code is and when you can and can't bill for it, who can bill for it, whether you bill the health insurance or you bill the mental side of it. They need to know also that the doctor does a visit, but then he does a test, too. You put the visit in, and you put the test in for the same date of service. The insurance company isn't going to pay for the visit unless they have a modifier code on there. Someone who doesn't have the experience with coding or any experience in medicine [isn't] going to know to put that code in to get that money for that doctor.

"Let's put this in another context: The family handyman sends his better half down to the building supply store with instructions to purchase a pound of 1½-inch drywall nails. When she gets there, the nice hardware man says drywall nails only come in 1 inch or 2¾-inch sizes. And the female half of the team—who's a mean cook but knows zippola about drywall—is left standing in the screw-and-nail aisle with no clue of what to do next.

"You can't just take the information that the doctor gives you," she adds emphatically. "You have to be able to analyze it and know what questions to ask and know how to fine-tune the information you get from the doctor."

The Denver MIB suggests that would-be medical billers with no prior experience take a job for a year with a billing service and learn from that. At least attend some one-day seminars on coding that are held in most cities so you can get a grasp of what kinds of things are going to be expected of you.

Starting Over

On the other side of the Great Debate fence, Mary V.—the former customer service engineer—explains how she geared up for her business and what sort of training and research she has in her battle chest.

"My background was with IBM. I'd been in that for close to 20 years and got downsized, like 56,000 others," Mary says. "Actually, I started as a customer engineer working on machines, which was unique in itself because women just didn't do that when I started. I was the fourth female hired in the Baltimore/Washington area to do that." By the end of her tenure, her beat was lease billing. "Basically, whenever billing time came around, I was on call, 24 hours a day."

Then came the downsizing. IBM offered its soon-to-be-ex-employees various classes in job placement and interviewing. One was in entrepreneurship. "A friend of mine and I said, 'Well, we've got to waste three days someplace, so let's go,'" recalls Mary.

A couple of programmers in the class had checked into medical billing, Mary remembers. "The more they talked over the three days, I thought, 'These two are the only ones who have a shot at making anything go.' And basically, that was it. I tucked that in the back of my mind. Once I left, I never thought about it again until I was told in a job interview that if I wasn't willing to work six months at a time or a year at a time, that I would never work again. And so I thought, 'Well, thank you very much, I don't want to do this again. I'll try something else.'

"That's when I started thinking about medical billing again. So that's how I got into it initially."

Mary purchased her first medical billing software package in 1993. "Then, as I got deeper and deeper into it, I found I needed to know a heck of a lot of stuff. So I took classes at the community colleges; any seminar that [came] up, I was there. Anywhere that I could get knowledge on this [industry], I would go. And I still go."

Today, after eight years, Mary has a client base of 14 providers. Not bad when you consider she had no medical background going into the business. You must also consider, however, that she set out to learn whatever she could at the outset.

My Friends, the Doctors

Curt J., the ministry-less pastor, began his business with no medical background, either. "Basically, I was playing with my computer at home, wasting a few hours a week. I needed extra income, so I began to research how I could meet the need and work with my computer, which I was having fun doing. So I basically just started looking on the internet for businesses, and I looked at *Entrepreneur* magazine and things like that. I kept boiling it down until finally I arrived at medical billing as the option I wanted to pursue."

After a great deal of research, he went with a business opportunity vendor in Arizona. After flying out for training, he returned home to get his fledgling operation off the ground. "I just started knocking on doors and visiting and sharing materials and so on and so forth," Curt says. "Now, I bill for one dentist and two chiropractors."

Although Curt had no medical background, he had friends in the business. "The reason I got into it," he says, "is a couple of my friends are doctors. One was a dentist, whom I'm billing for. I didn't want to deal with just the general masses and marketing or retail or anything like that. That's part of what appealed to me, too; the clientele are business owners, office managers, and doctors."

But he echoes the sentiments of everyone on both sides of the Great Debate. "In my opinion there's no way you can just buy software and get into this business. I made dozens of phone calls—and still do—back to [the business opportunity]," says Curt. "I can't imagine anybody just buying the software and doing this, unless they have a lot of medical background."

▲

Summing Up

So, like ladies and gentlemen of the jury in a celebrated court case, you've heard both sides of the argument. To sum up, one side stands firm that without a medical background, you're asking for trouble. The other side stands as proof that a background in medicine or medical billing is not a prerequisite for MIB success.

You should note, however, that both sides agree on an important issue: If you don't have a medical background, you must be willing to work hard in your new field. You must take into account a major learning curve.

You can succeed—brilliantly—but you have to be willing to pay the piper.

The Prognosis

If you're still reading, we assume you've decided to take the MIB challenge and forge ahead with your new career. There is, however, one more thing to take into consideration: the industry prognosis. Will medical billing be around as technical advances unfold in the 21st century?

The future looks good. As we saw at the start of the chapter, there's a great big beautiful tomorrow for the health-care industry. Unless a meteor from outer space crashes into Earth, or unless aliens from the planet Zark land on the White House lawn and show us how to eradicate injury and illness for all time, the industry outlook is healthy.

It is possible that a national health-care plan will finally come to pass and the manner in which health-care is billed and paid for could change. Doctors, however, will still have to be paid, and patients will still have to file claims. Somebody will still have to file them, and who better than the MIB?

So, fasten your seat belt, bring your tray table to the upright position, and let's start your learning curve. Next chapter: Health Insurance 101!

Health Insurance 101

There's much more to medical billing than meets the eye. Even though the CMS 1500 mainstreamed the claim form, the MIB's world is full of corporate and governmental entities whose main goal in life often appears to be obstructing easy claims processing.

As World War II posters frequently reminded: "Know your enemy." Keeping up with changes—an important part of the medical billing industry—is easier when you understand where insurers are going, as well as where they've been.

It's also extremely necessary to speak the lingo, to be able to rattle off information about carriers, administrators, beneficiaries, and comprehensive plans and actually know what you're talking about.

Who's Who in Insurance

The Carrier. This may sound as if it is referring to someone you'd rather not get up close and personal with, like Typhoid Mary, but in fact it refers to the insurance company that writes and administers the insurance policy. The carrier is also known as the *insurer, underwriter,* or *administrator.*

Each carrier can offer a variety of insurance plans. A single carrier might sell individual policies and group policies and administer a federal program such as Medicare. These plans—which can be worded as craftily as a government foreign aid policy—fall into three basic groups:

1. *Individual policies.* These are purchased by (surprise!) individuals rather than by or for groups, although they can cover an individual and spouse, or an individual and family. Homeowners and vehicle insurance policies also provide health-care benefits to cover, for example, an auto accident, a dog bite, or a fall on a frozen front walk.

2. *Group policies.* This is the package deal concept. Most group policies are provided by employers for their employees. In some cases, it's a freebie; in others, the employees pay for the insurance with the idea that their cost is lower than it would be if they purchased the policy on their own. Group policies are also purchased by (surprise!) groups for their members, such as the Romance Writers of America or the Good Sam Club.

3. *Government programs.* Although Medicare, Medicaid, and Civilian Health and Medical Program for the Uniformed Services (CHAMPUS) are government entities, they are administered by the private sector—insurance companies or data processing firms.

The Provider. This refers to the person who provides health-care services and/or supplies. A provider can be a physician, pharmacist, physical therapist, outside laboratory performing various tests, or a medical supply company that rents or sells wheelchairs or walkers. In the medical office, the doctor is considered the provider even when it is the nurse or assistant who draws the blood or performs the test.

The Beneficiary. This is the person eligible to receive benefits under the health insurance policy; simply, the patient.

The Insured. This is the policy holder, the person who is covered by the insurance program and who makes it possible for his or her family to be covered. In other words, the insured is the employee whose employment makes the group coverage available. The insured can also be referred to as the *enrollee, certificate holder*, or *subscriber.*

The Dependents. These are the children and spouse—or in some areas the significant other—of the insured. Policies define covered dependents using these criteria:

- The insured's spouse must not be legally separated from the insured and must not be in the armed forces.

- A dependent child must be the insured's unmarried child (including any step-child, legally adopted child, or foster child); must not be a member of the armed forces; and, if older than 19 but younger than 23, shall be considered a dependent only if not employed on a full-time basis and if living at the insured's home address. (See what we mean about policy-speak?)

- A child who is physically or mentally incapable of self-support at the age of 23 may continue to be covered while remaining incapacitated and unmarried.

Get with the Group

Group insurance frequently takes the form of a self-insured plan. In this type of program, the employer, rather than an insurance company, provides the funds to pay its employees' claims. Simple, you say. But wait! It then often hires a TPA *(third-party administrator)* to administer the plan. The TPA can be an insurance company or a specialized management company. Sometimes this employer/administrator arrangement is called an ASO, for *administrative services only.*

Or, it can take the guise of an MPP, which stands for *minimum premium plan.* In these plans, the employer goes the self-insurance route up to a certain dollar amount and then pays a commercial carrier to take on the risk for everything over and above that sum.

The Exclusive Exclusion List

When an individual or group buys health insurance, the contract between the purchaser and the carrier spells out the coverage provided, as well as the limitations of that coverage. The more limits there are, the lower the cost to the purchaser. The insurer is obligated to cover (and provide reimbursement for) only those services specified in the contract. Here are some of the general factors that limit this coverage:

○ *Listed exclusions.* A policy can list specific services, procedures, and/or supplies as being excluded from coverage; for example, maternity care, dental care, or surgery to implant the Hope Diamond as a permanent wrist ornament. No benefits will be paid for listed exclusions.

○ *Pre-existing conditions.* Depending on the terms of the policy, coverage for the treatment of pre-existing conditions may also be excluded or limited.

○ *Maximums.* Most policies will pay specific maximum dollar amounts. These can concern a specific illness or be annual or lifetime maximums.

○ *Annual maximum.* If a policy has an annual coverage maximum, it will pay no more than that amount in a benefit year or calendar year, depending on the terms of the policy.

○ *Lifetime maximum.* This one's not quite what it sounds like. Some policies do not completely exclude certain conditions but will discontinue coverage for them once they've paid a specific maximum amount, a sort of "OK, Bub, we've had enough" clause.

○ *Mental and addictive disorders.* Insurance policies routinely include separate schedules of benefits for mental, psychoneurotic, and personality disorders, and for the treatment of drug and alcohol addictions. These items might be excluded entirely, or they might be subject to limitations.

○ *Deductible.* The amount and type of deductible depend on the policy, with the deductible usually directly related to the premium. The insured may opt for a higher deductible in exchange for a lower premium, or he may go for a plan with no deductible that specifies care from certain providers.

○ *Individual/family deductible.* In some policies, each covered family member must meet his or her own deductible. In others, all the family's expenses go toward a single deductible.

○ *Co-insurance.* This standard provision requires the insured to share the cost of certain covered services. The insured must pay either a set fee for a given service or a specified percentage of the cost of that service.

Now that we have established who the players are, let's look at who is making the rules. There are more than 2,000 health insurance carriers in the United States, with three or four times as many plans. Health insurance coverage falls into six categories: commercial, Blue Cross or Blue Shield (called the Blues, or BCBS), Medicare, Medicaid, CHAMPUS, and workers' compensation.

Commercial Carriers

Commercial carriers offer health insurance contracts to individuals and groups. Think the big traditionals—Aetna, Humana, and United Healthcare—for an idea of what we are talking about here. But, of course, there are thousands of smaller carriers as well. As opposed to various altruistic government or nonprofit carriers, commercial carriers are in the health insurance business to make money.

Some commercial plans are *indemnity* policies. This does not refer to the classic Fred MacMurray film about murder to collect life insurance but rather to the fact that the carrier *indemnifies* or reimburses the patient for covered services up to a limit set in the policy. For example, it might pay for mental health services up to a yearly limit of $1,000 or a lifetime limit or cap of $10,000. This type of plan assumes that the patient is going to pay the doctor when services are rendered.

Fun Fact
The U.S. Census Bureau, self-proclaimed "pre-eminent collector and provider of timely, relevant, and quality data," conducted its first survey in 1790. On the medical time line, this was just six years before Dr. Edward Jenner developed the smallpox vaccine.

Then there's the policy that bypasses the patient and sends the check directly to the doctor. For the provider, this is a sort of good news/bad news option. The good news, of course, is that the physician receives direct payment; the bad news is that the doctor is paid in accordance with what the carrier considers *usual and customary* fees, which might not necessarily be what the doctor considers fair compensation.

To make matters more complicated—or more interesting, if you're a glass-half-full instead of half-empty type—various policies limit coverage to various disorders or types of service. Some might not cover maternity services, others might exclude mental disorders, and still others might not allow treatment by chiropractors, optometrists, or dentists.

Those Dang Deductibles

The *deductible* is the amount the patient must pay before the insurance coverage kicks in. If the policy specifies a $500 deductible, for example, and the patient racks up $600 worth of medical expenses, the carrier will pay toward the last $100, leaving the

I'll Have the Usual

In the cozy world of the coffee shop or diner, "the usual" means what the customer always orders. In the often obtuse world of health insurance, "the usual" is something different. Usual, customary, and reasonable (UCR) refers to a method of regulating health-care costs. Under the UCR method, insurers pay providers as little as they can, or rather, the lesser of these three schedules:

○ *Usual fee.* The usual or normal amount doctors charge for a specific service. This figure is determined by insurers who keep annual tabs and then compute an average fee.

○ *Customary fee.* This one is determined by insurers based on 90 percent of the fees charged by all doctors in the same specialty in the same geographic region.

○ *Reasonable fee.* Here we have the least of: a) the fee the doctor has actually billed, b) the usual fee, c) the customary fee, or d) some other specially justifiable fee.

Another even more complicated method of determining fees is the RBRVS, which, in English, is the Resource-Based Relative Value Scale. Developed by the Harvard School of Public Health, the RBRVS uses all of the following items to come up with a reasonable charge: a) the actual amount of work performed by the doctor; b) the doctor's expenses, excluding malpractice insurance; and c) the cost of malpractice insurance.

Now, just in case you thought that was easy, the RBRVS system multiplies each of these items by an index based on geographic areas and then multiplies the total by a conversion factor decided upon by Congress to account for inflation.

How did Congress get in there? The system was developed at the federal government's behest as a response to Medicare's runaway expenditures.

patient to take care of the balance. If the patient is a basically healthy type and never reaches the $500 mark, the insurance company isn't going to cough up a dime.

Most policies have an *allowable* amount for covered services. This means the insurer pays a portion—usually 70 to 80 percent—of the doctor's fee, and the patient pays the balance, which is called the *co-payment* or *co-insurance*. If the policy above has a $500 deductible and the allowable amount is 80 percent, the insurance carrier will pay $80 of the total $600 bill. (And you thought you were through with word problems!)

In deference to the insured who's having a run of poor health, many policies also include a stop-loss provision, which limits the total co-payments the policy holder must make in a given year. Once the insured has paid $1,000 in co-payments, for example, the carrier forgoes any further co-payments and picks up 100 percent of the tab for any and all remaining covered services.

The Big Three

There are three main types of commercial insurance plans.

- *Basic.* These plans pay total costs up to a maximum (usually around $5,000) for all but a few exclusions such as cosmetic surgery and mental disorders. They might or might not have a deductible. Costs can be incurred in the hospital, at the doctor's office, or at home.

- *Major medical.* These policies are designed for catastrophic situations such as extended hospitalization, which might give you another major medical catastrophe if you saw the bill and didn't have the insurance coverage. They don't pay for minor health problems or office visits, and they almost always feature large deductibles and co-payments.

- *Comprehensive.* These plans, the combo plate on the commercial carrier's menu, are composites of both basic and major medical coverage.

Stat Fact
According to a recent U.S. Census Bureau report, most of us (249 million people) are covered by a private insurance plan. More than 27.3 percent of Americans have some form of government coverage in the form of Medicare, Medicaid, or military care. Many people have the combo plate, with more than one of the above.

The Blues

Blue Cross and Blue Shield are the hallmarks of American prepaid health-care coverage. They have been in existence, in one form or another, since the teens of the 20th century. Together, they now provide health insurance coverage to more than one in three Americans, more than 98 million people.

According to the Blue Cross–Blue Shield, the group offers a variety of products, with 65.8 million folks in a PPO plan, 12.9 million in a fee-for-service program, 15.8 million in an HMO, and 4.8 million in a point-of-service (POS) plan. Blue Cross–Blue Shield is the largest single processor of Medicare claims in the United States.

Blue Cross was originally developed to pay hospitalization costs, while Blue Shield's purpose was to pay for doctors' services. Now, both "brands," as the parent organization likes to call them, have in most states merged into a single entity, the Blue Cross–Blue Shield System.

Blue Cross came along in 1929 when Justin Ford Kimball, an official at Baylor University in Dallas, Texas, ushered in a plan to give schoolteachers 21 days of hospital care for just $6 a year. (The current equivalent would be about $35 a year.)

Split Personality

When a patient is covered under two or more health insurance policies, he is said to have dual coverage. This phenomenon is not unusual, especially in today's both-spouses-bringing-home-the-bacon families. Here are some tips on the twin policy front:

○ *Group plans.* Group health insurance plans usually include a *coordination of benefits* clause. Also known as *nonduplication of benefits,* this provision states that when a patient is covered by more than one group plan, the total benefits paid by all policies are limited to 100 percent of the actual charges.

○ *Birthday rule.* When a dependent is covered under multiple group plans because both parents have coverage through their employers, the parents' dates of birth are used to determine which coverage is primary, with the older parent's taking first position. Like the old first aid test question of "Where do you put the tourniquet if the patient is snakebit on the neck?" you could beg the question of what happens if both parents have the same birth date. You might or might not get an answer.

○ *Government plans.* If a patient has dual coverage and one of the plans is Medicaid, the government plan is considered supplementary to the private or group plan. Medicare is the major exception here since so many of its insureds also have Medigap coverage. In this case, of course, Medicare is the primary policy. On the other hand, however, for seniors who are still working after age 65 and have both a group and Medicare policy, the group policy counts as the primary.

Other employee groups in Dallas decided the teachers were onto a good thing and jumped on the bandwagon. The idea quickly attracted attention nationwide.

The program snowballed from there, adopting the Blue Cross symbol in 1939, the same year the first modern Blue Shield plan was founded in California. In 10 years, the plan grew from 1,300 participants to 3 million. Now, at the beginning of the new millennium, the Blue Cross–Blue Shield System is one of the largest employers in the United States, processes the most hospital and physician contracts, sells insurance to all sectors of the health-care market; and offers 39 plans in all 50 states, the District of Columbia, and Puerto Rico.

Alphabet Soup

At this point, you might be asking yourself "Just what the heck are HMOs and PPOs?"

HMO stands for *Health Maintenance Organization* and is a sort of privatized version of a national health-care plan. There are various permutations of HMOs, but the gist is that patients pay a monthly fee to belong, much as they would with Blue Cross–Blue Shield. When they need medical care, they present a card like a credit card or library card instead of a claim form. They then see a preassigned physician, called the *primary* physician, within the organization and pay either a nominal fee per visit or no fee at all.

> **Fun Fact**
> On the medical movie time line, 1939 was a big year for films as well as health insurance—everybody went to see *Calling Dr. Kildare* and *The Secret of Dr. Kildare*.

The HMO system insists that the patient see only her primary doctor. She can't choose another doctor within the HMO and she certainly can't pick one out of the phone book or because Mrs. Hoodle down the street recommended him. HMOs also demand that patients see a specialist only upon the authorization and referral of the primary physician.

The upside of the HMO system is that because the organization is trying to whittle down major medical costs by concurrently whittling away at major medical problems, it will pay for a lot of preventive services (such as well-baby checkups, well-adult physicals, mammograms, and immunizations) that traditional fee-for-service carriers won't cover.

Because of all the taboos, however, HMOs receive a lot of flak from the public, who often feel that their power of choice has been taken away and that the HMO is not providing optimal care. Doctors are not wild about HMOs, either, for the same reasons and for many others, including, of course, money.

Providers who work for HMOs are usually paid on a *capitation* basis. This has nothing to do with decapitating people, but stems from the same root word and refers to the practice of counting heads. The HMO decides how many patients the doctor is likely to see in his office in a given month and then pays him for treating that number regardless of how many patients actually cross his threshold.

Regardless, it seems the HMO is here to stay, along with its kissing cousin, the *PPO*, or *Preferred Provider Organization*. This is a group of doctors who cooperate with an insurance plan by accepting fee-for-service payments at less than the usual and customary rate. Unlike most of their HMO brethren, PPO doctors are allowed to see nonplan patients and charge their own fees. PPO patients are granted more autonomy as well and can choose a doctor outside the plan, although they then have to pay a larger chunk of the bill.

Swimming around in the alphabet soup of *managed care organizations* are a bevy of other crossbreeds. There is the *IPA*, or *Independent Practice Association*; the *EPO*, or *Exclusive Provider Organization*; the *POS*, or *Point of Service plan*; and the *MSO*, otherwise known as the *Managed Service Organization*.

So long as you don't confuse MSO with MSG or IPA with the IRA, you should be able to wade your way through this lot. As with all other insurance plans, the important thing to be aware of is what and how the particular plan pays the physician.

Muddling through Medicare

Medicare began in 1965 as a star player in President Lyndon B. Johnson's "Great Society," which stemmed from his belief that every American should be able to partake of

> **Fun Fact**
> You can access just about anything you'd ever want to know about the Blues, including a mind-boggling array of statistics, on the association's Web site at www.bluecares.com. You can also check out Blue TV and Blue Radio on the site for speeches and discussions from leading experts in the health-care field.

our nation's wealth. The federal government's gift to older Americans in the form of health insurance, Medicare is available to almost everyone who has reached the grand age of 65. Younger people who suffer from end-stage renal disease (ESRD) and/or have been collecting Social Security disability benefits for more than two years are also eligible.

The Social Security Administration handles Medicare enrollment and premium collection, but the program itself is run by CMS (the agency, not the form). Keep in mind, however, that claims billing is handled by various commercial carriers such as the Blues, called *intermediaries*, and that these carriers vary among states.

Medicare consists of two parts: Part A and (surprise!) Part B. You can think of them as Hospital and Medical, despite the government's delight in obscure appellations.

- *Part A.* This section provides insurance for inpatient hospital services including skilled nursing facilities, hospices, and home health care.
- *Part B.* This portion covers doctors' services, outpatient hospital care, X-rays, lab tests, ambulance services, durable medical equipment, and other nonhospitalization services.

> **Fun Fact**
> What do aircraft carriers and baby boomers have in common? Henry Kaiser, the father of both mass-produced Navy ships during World War II and the Kaiser Permanente Health Plan.

Everyone who has worked, or whose spouse has worked, in Medicare-covered employment or self-employment (basically everybody who had taxes deducted from their pay) for at least 10 years is entitled to freebie Part A coverage. Those who don't qualify for the freebie can often purchase Part A coverage; for example, people under age 65 who are disabled but no longer receive disability benefits because of their earnings.

Everyone entitled to Part A is also entitled to Part B—for a price. The monthly premium is usually deducted directly from the insured's monthly Social Security check. There is also a yearly deductible for Part B coverage, after which Medicare pays 80 percent of the approved amount for all covered services and the patient pays the remaining 20 percent, or *co-insurance*. Sort of.

If the charges are for outpatient hospital services, the insured pays 20 percent of whatever the hospital charges, not 20 percent of the amount approved by Medicare. If the outpatient service was for a mental health problem, the insured pays 50 percent of the Medicare-approved amount. You can visit www.cms.gov for information about deductibles.

Part B Particulars

The most important thing to remember about Part B coverage is that it covers doctor's bills, no matter where they're incurred—at home, in the doctor's office, in a

Back to HMOs

Most Medicare beneficiaries who belong to HMOs do not bother their little heads with Medicare's deductibles or co-insurance amounts (although they still make co-payments to the HMO), and they still receive all the perks of Medicare coverage. But—and this is a big but—the HMO to which they belong probably has a cost contract with Medicare, which means there are lock-in requirements. Which, in turn, means that the Medicare patient is locked into receiving all her care from that particular HMO. Medicare will not pay for any services from any outside source unless it's during an emergency or while the patient is away from the plan's service area.

If the patient belongs to a POS, or point-of-service type of HMO, he probably has enrolled under a *cost plan*. In this case, he is allowed to go to providers outside the managed care plan and Medicare will pay its share of the bill. In this case, however, the patient is responsible for Medicare's co-insurance and deductibles.

The savvy MIB keeps all these factors in mind when billing for Medicare providers. It's complicated, but it can be fun, too. It's all a game, and the more you know, the more you can win for your doctors, as well as for their patients.

▲

clinic, or even, presumably, on the golf course. The doctor's fees for services rendered in the hospital or nursing home are also covered here, as opposed to Part A coverage for the charges from the hospital or nursing home itself.

Part B also covers the following:

- Outpatient hospital services
- X-rays and diagnostic tests
- Certain ambulance services
- Durable medical equipment used at home, such as wheelchairs and hospital beds
- Services of certain nonphysician practitioners
- Physical and occupational therapy
- Speech/language pathology services
- Partial hospitalization for mental health care
- Mammograms and Pap smears
- Some home health care

For would-be Draculas, Part B covers blood after the patient has met the annual deductible of three pints. It usually doesn't cover outpatient prescription drugs, but it makes an exception for some oral anticancer drugs, certain drugs for hospice patients, and those that are administered as part of the doctor's services. It also covers various drugs given in the first year after transplant surgery, epoetin for home dialysis patients, antigens and flu, pneumococcal and hepatitis B vaccines.

Accepting Assignment

If all of the above brings back awful memories of your high school algebra book, don't panic. It's a lot to swallow now, but as you flex your MIB wings and use your skills, Medicare's little rules will become second nature.

Feeling better? Good—because now we need to discuss more math, aka "Fun with Accepting Assignment."

First up: The amount Medicare will pay for a covered service is the lesser of two evils, er, the lesser of two prices: Medicare's preapproved amount or the amount charged by the provider. For example, let's say Medicare allows $100 for a simple wart removal. Let's also say Dr. Whosit, who likes to call his own shots, thinks his wart removal services are worth more.

Smart Tip

The CMS people will send you their Guide to Health Insurance for People with Medicare for free if you call (800) 633-4227 or log onto www.medicare.gov to download the PDF. This handy booklet—designed for the beneficiary but great reading for the MIB—gives all sorts of Medicare information in a clear, no-nonsense format and should be an important part of your library.

Now, if Dr. Whosit accepts assignment from Medicare—meaning he will accept Medicare's approved wart fee as his full payment—he bills Medicare for $100. Medicare sends a check for $80 (80 percent of $100) directly to him, and he bills the patient for the remaining $20, which is the other 20 percent, or co-insurance amount. End of story.

If, on the other hand, Dr. Whosit does not accept assignment, he bills the patient $115. Why this amount? Because doctors who do not accept assignment are allowed to charge up to 15 percent more than the Medicare-approved amount and no more. This is referred to as the *limiting charge*.

By law, Dr. Whosit must also send a bill to Medicare on the patient's behalf, but Medicare will send the payment—which is still only $80 (Medicare's 80 percent of the approved $100 amount)—to the patient. The patient will then remember that he owes this $80, plus the remaining $35, to Dr. Whosit and fire off a check.

Benefit Basics

An *EOB* is an *Explanation of Benefits* and is the insurance carrier's method of summarizing the details of the claim submitted and explaining the particulars of reimbursement. Although each payer can define benefits in its own endearingly idiosyncratic way, you can expect to find essentially the same information on any EOB:

- ○ Patient's name and relationship to insured
- ○ Services rendered, dates of service and total charges
- ○ Exclusions and special (not sarcastic, although it may seem that way) remarks about the reason for denial, suspended claims, or additional information needed
- ○ Amount of total charges covered
- ○ Deductible amounts due for each service
- ○ Percentage of allowed balance paid
- ○ Required provider adjustments or other deductions

▲

Now, let's say Dr. Whosit's brother, Dr. Whatsit, does his wart removals for only $80 a pop. Medicare will pay $64, which is 80 percent of $80, and Dr. Whatsit can bill his patient $16, which is the remaining 20 percent. Got it? Good.

Now, one more interesting twist. Let's say Dr. Whosit has a colleague, Dr. Frankenstein. And let's say Dr. Frank is running a laboratory (as in diagnostic lab testing). Medicare will require Dr. Frank to accept assignment—he has no choice in the matter.

As a last aside, you should know that doctors decide each year whether or not to take the plunge and accept assignment. If they do, they become a *PAR* or *participating physician* (guess Medicare decided the acronym PP wouldn't be too appealing). If they decline, they become a *non-PAR*.

Oh, That Medigap!

Many purchase supplemental health-care insurance to cover co-insurance fees. This supplemental coverage is referred to as *Medigap* because it fills in the gaps between what Medicare pays and what it doesn't.

Medigap insurance is sold and administered by private carriers, but it is regulated by both state and federal laws. There are ten standard plans, lettered A through J (one through ten would be too easy), and insurers are not allowed to sell more than these ten plans. Plan A is the basic package and must be offered, although, of course, purchasers can go with the upgrade of their choice.

Medigap policies cover all, or nearly all, co-insurance amounts. Some cover deductibles. Others pay doctor charges that exceed the approved amount, and still others take care of otherwise noncovered services such as prescription drugs and preventive screenings (the health-care kind, not the Hollywood movie kind).

Let's go back to Dr. Whosit and let's say he's accepting Medicare assignment. Let's say that you, his ace medical biller, put the patient's Medigap policy number on the Medicare claim and send it in. Medicare will process the claim and then automatically forward it to the Medigap carrier, which will process the claim and send a check directly to Dr. W.

Even keener, some Medigap insurers have *cross-over contracts* with Medicare. In these cases, Medicare will automatically forward claims even if the doctor does not accept assignment.

Medicaid

The Medicaid program is designed to provide health-care coverage for people residing at or near the poverty level—people who could not otherwise afford any health care at all. Administered jointly by CMS and each state's government, the program has one major flaw—its allowable charges are pitifully low, from 35 percent to 50 percent of the usual and customary fees. Most doctors don't accept Medicaid because the cost of doing the paperwork, not to mention the costs of providing the service, exceed the amount they'll be paid.

Some patients have Medicare as their primary coverage and Medicaid as supplemental health-care coverage. These people are called *crossover patients*. Like Medicare, Medicaid claims are processed by private carriers, and these carriers vary among states.

> ### Smart Tip
>
> *The Medicare Guide* (available from CMS at 800-633-4227 or www.medicare.gov) contains a dandy chart detailing the benefits of each Medigap plan.

CHAMPUS

Moving right along on the government insurance hit parade, we arrive at CHAMPUS, which is an acronym for Civilian Health and Medical Program of the Uniformed Services. CHAMPUS provides civilian health-care coverage to active and retired military personnel and their dependents so they can be treated by George Clooney instead of Captain Newman, M.D.

CHAMPUS is similar in most respects to Medicare, except that it has different deductibles and co-payments and pays a greater percentage of provider fees. When a CHAMPUS beneficiary reaches age 65, he or she is—whoosh—transferred to the Medicare program.

Workers' Compensation

This used to be called work*men's* compensation insurance until gender equality struck. *Workers'* compensation provides private insurance coverage for both males and females who become injured or ill while on the job and can encompass everything from a knock on the noggin with a steel beam to stress-related mental illness.

Every employer with more than a specific number of employees is required by law to carry workers' compensation insurance, which is provided—at a staggering price—by various private carriers.

Workers' comp cases are handled differently from most other insurance claims. Sometimes it's unclear if the case even is a workers' comp matter. For example, an employee involved in an auto accident may have been tooling around in the company car on her off time, or a stress-related problem may stem from a tyrannical spouse instead of the boss from hell. In such an instance, second-opinion reviews may be required. This can also occur in cases involving a dispute about the level of disability.

Treatment must be preauthorized (the insurance carrier must be called while the patient bleeds onto the emergency room floor, unless, of course, it's after hours for the

▲

Associating with the Medical Billing Industry

Liz Jones, academic director for the Medical Association of Billers, has some advice for anyone hoping to get involved in the medical billing business—don't quit your day job . . . yet. "To me, you really have to know the different types of insurance," Jones says. "I suggest people work six months to a year in a doctor's office before they start a business." That way, she says, you work and earn money while enjoying a ramp-up period.

Jones knows her stuff, so it's wise to trust her advice. As academic director for the MAB, she helps create programming and learning opportunities for around 1500 members worldwide. The MAB was founded in 1995 in Las Vegas, and the association web site launched in 1997. It was one of the first groups to offer online classes, which they still do, along with facetime learning opportunities. The group's Power Weekends provide medical billers with a two-day refresher course on coding and billing. The MAB also offers on-site training at your place of business, certification training, proctor sites, and a national conference for billing professionals.

"This is a good business, but you have to pay your dues," Jones says. As such, she does not necessarily recommend the "turnkey" approach to starting your own billing service. The software required, she says, is often too complicated for an inexperienced novice to get used to immediately. "It's not as easy as sitting down at the computer and plugging in numbers," she says. There are nuances of each insurance company and each medical office that one must master in order to bill the most money for her clients. So, do your homework first and participate in as many professional activities as you can prior to hanging out your shingle, from working in a medical office to taking a certification class.

Challenges are many for the first-time MIB, the biggest of which is getting that first client. If working full-time in a medical office isn't a possibility for you, Jones says to offer some of your time as a volunteer for a physician's office to see if you enjoy the environment and pace of work. "Most people will spend money [on software] before they get a client. It's a shame to put that kind of money into it when you don't even know if you like doing it." Once you do get that first client, focus plenty of energy on recruiting new clients. Jones recommends starting with people you know. One client has a lot of marketing power if he tells his colleagues about his good experience with you, so don't be afraid to ask for referrals. Jones predicts that you will need at least three or four clients to really start bringing in some solid funds. "If you just have one small contractor," she says, "I wouldn't quit your day job."

To find out more about the Medical Association of Billers, visit their web site at www.physicianweb sites.com. There, you'll find tons of resources from forms and sample documents to HIPAA information and member forums.

insurer, in which case a call is put in as soon after treatment as possible). After treatment, the provider must fill out lots of other fun forms, such as the Initial Medical Report and the First Report of Injury. These reports must include the case number and the adjuster's name.

Fee allowances are set by the state and paid directly to the doctor by the insurance carrier.

The End, Finito

There are so many rules, regulations, permutations, and ins and outs in insurance coverage that this chapter could easily stretch on forever.

What we have provided should give you a good basic grounding in Insurance 101. The rest you can learn in several ways:

- *Immerse yourself.* There is no better way to learn than by throwing yourself into the deep end.
- *Send away for stuff.* Remember when you were a kid and you sent away for free stuff out of magazines, just to get something in the mail? Well, you can still do it. Only now you can send away for stuff that you really need, such as the *Medicare Guide*. We have provided a list of helpful goodies you can use in Appendix A.
- *Ask for help.* Answers are out there for the asking. Develop a network of MIB buddies. Get on the internet with everybody from fellow billers to the Blues. Go to your business opportunity or software vendor.
- *Demand answers.* There's no better source for answers than the problem itself. You can always call Medicare or Blue Cross or the CHAMPUS carrier and tell them what you need to know. Ask nicely—but firmly.

Day to Day
Operations

Now that you are versed in the ins and outs and whys and wherefores of health insurance, let's take a look at operations. In this chapter, we explore what an MIB's work life is really like, what sorts of tasks you can expect to perform on a daily basis and how they are completed. If Chapter 1 was akin to investigative reports, then Chapter 3 is a text-only version of all those big coffee-table books called *A Day in the Life of Spam or Delaware: An Intimate Portrait.* You know, the ones that show every facet of the subject's life from rising at dawn to feed the chickens to midnight fireworks over the Capitol.

As a rule, MIBs don't actually dabble in animal husbandry, but since many are stay-at-home moms as well as business owners, they do often rise at dawn's early light to do a little work before feeding their hungry chicks. Our version of *A Day in the Life* won't feature midnight "fireworks"—but we will peer into nightly routines and rituals.

Good Morning, Medical Biller!

One of the great joys of running a medical billing service is that you can arrange your workload around any schedule you choose. Some MIBs are early birds, catching those worms; others find they get more accomplished in the afternoon or at night. The hours they spend and the time frames within which they structure those hours are as individual as each entrepreneur.

"The funniest thing," says an MIB in New Jersey, and the mother of two, "is that most people who are trying to get in the business and have talked to me, really want me to answer the question as to how many hours a day I work. I just can never answer that because I don't know."

She may have 20 minutes to sit down, undisturbed, she explains, before she may be called upon to get up, fix lunch, and get the kids off to school. Then she can come back and work for an hour, but something always comes up. "It's never-ending," she says.

"Of course, [my daily schedule is] always changing," says the former nurse/MIB in San Diego who's also a mother of two. "I tend to get up early in the morning because that is my peace-and-quiet time. So I'm usually up by 5:30 in the morning, in my office by 6:00."

If your eyes roll back in your head at the idea of rising before Good Morning America appears on the tube, don't panic. This is not an industry must. "My mornings are pretty much my most hectic time," the New Jersey MIB explains. She does the mommy stuff in between taking client calls and fielding problems. "Most of my clients pretty much know my schedule and they know that the mornings are for troubleshooting."

She breaks near noon for lunch, bundles the kids off to kindergarten and day care, then, she says, "I pretty much have from 12:30 P.M. to 4:00 P.M. where I can really sit and work."

Beware!
When you work at home, friends and family can monopolize your time, dropping in for a cup of coffee and a chat because "you're home anyway." Be polite but firm. Let them know you're at the office and need to buckle down to business.

Practice Particulars

What, specifically, you will be doing during your peak hours and beyond will depend on how you've structured your services. Some MIBs perform *full practice management* for their clients—they handle all aspects of the doctor's accounting from submitting electronic claims to billing patients to tracking accounts payable and receivable. Other medical billers prefer to deal only with insurance claims submissions. Most MIBs, being savvy businesspeople, take on whatever is required to land the client and therefore find themselves working in different ranges of practice management for different clients.

The How-To Revue

Here's the Radio City Rockettes' chorus line of chores, a sort of rapid-fire revue of an MIB's daily bump and grind:

1. Enter your patient information, adding new insurance carriers to your database as you go along. Be sure you enter the referral source or referring physician as well as any other information you've agreed to track for your clients.

2. Enter CPT and ICD-10 codes from the superbills and day sheets. Your software will automatically fill in the amounts charged for each procedure. Enter each charge on a separate line.

3. Transmit electronic claims directly to insurance carriers or to the clearinghouse.

4. Receive audit report, review, and correct errors on audit report, forward clean claims, and resubmit rejected claims.

5. Print any paper claims. Separate claims into your copy and the insurer's, fold, and insert in envelopes. Weigh any envelopes containing more than five claims to make sure you have sufficient postage.

6. Post payments to each patient's account. Most software programs include features that show which charges have been paid, how much is left on each charge and which charges are still unpaid.

7. Print aging reports so you can review each patient's account to determine which ones haven't been paid in a timely manner. Most software packages will do this for you, too.

8. Call insurance carriers to check on the status of delinquent claims. Most of your follow-up calls will be for paper claims.

9. Put your feet up and relax. You've earned a breather.

▲

"I'm kind of an à la carte," the Denver MIB says of the services she offers. ["The doctors] just tell me what kind of services they need. That's what I try to provide and then I charge them accordingly."

Mary V. discovered that smaller practices, those with one or two doctors at the helm, have no business background and desperately need assistance. "I don't like to say full-practice management," Mary says of the accounting services she offers these small practices, "because we're not in that office. We call it accounts receivable management."

In western Virginia, Kim H. prefers to stick to claims billing, but she also does patient billing for two of her four providers simply because they requested the service. Her reasoning? "I didn't want to turn them down."

The Nitty-Gritty

Most software packages are equipped to handle as many billing tasks as you care to take on. In addition to claims billing and patient accounting, many allow you to spew out a dazzling variety of reports and graphs. You can chart each provider's income by type of insurance carrier or by how much income she's derived from each referring physician. You can also punch out all the normal sorts of accounting reports.

The Denver MIB provides each of her doctors with a monthly report, which she breaks down between office and hospital production or between inpatient and outpatient services. The report details all the doctor's procedures and how many times those procedures were performed, then goes on to chart collections, which she breaks down into special categories such as medical records copying, legal arbitrations, and depositions.

No matter how esoteric you want to get, your most basic task will be generating and transmitting insurance claims. Software makes this part a snap. Although each program has its own variations, the basic setup is the same, featuring a screen or screens where you enter the patient's particulars, including name, phone, address, policy number, date of injury or illness, the diagnosis and procedure codes, and the doctor's charges.

When you first take on a practice, you'll spend a fair number of hours entering all the doctor's patients into your program. Although this is a time-consuming kickoff, it's well worth the effort—afterward you'll always have most of the information you'll need on file. Unless established patients move or change employers or insurance companies, all you'll need to fill in are the details of the illness or injury, the diagnosis and procedure codes, and the charges. The basics—name, address, phone, employer, policy number(s), insured family member's name and relationship, your own file or ID number for the patient—are already entered.

Sometimes the diagnosis portion is pretty simple, too. Chiropractors, for example, tend to treat the same problem for an extended period, so once you have Patient

Peterson down for a wrenched back diagnosis, that code will remain the same until the patient finishes his course of treatment.

Secret Decoder Ring

At this point you might be thinking "Gee, swell! Except where in the heck do I get the codes?"

Insurer, May I?

Insurance carriers often require providers to obtain precertification before they'll agree to pay for certain hospital admissions, inpatient or outpatient surgeries, and elective procedures (ones not requiring immediate action). Precertification was designed to reduce health-care costs by reducing or eliminating unnecessary services; therefore, the doctor must inform the carrier of the medical service planned and receive permission before forging ahead.

Most Medicaid programs have rigid precertification requirements for all nonemergency hospitalizations and surgeries. Most commercial plans now follow suit, insisting on precertification for nonemergency hospitalizations and for specific surgical procedures such as tonsillectomies.

As an added bonus, many carriers require the doctor to produce a second opinion before they'll approve the procedure or course of treatment. Some offer employers reduced premiums in return for revised plans that include some precertification clauses.

With more than 2,000 commercial and government carriers out there, you can't know every stipulation for every carrier. You'll learn by trial and error and from others' experiences.

Offer your doctors a "Precertification Form" to use in their practices. This is a great marketing technique, as well as smart business sense. It shows your clients your knowledge and efficiency while it streamlines operations.

You can copy the form on page 43 or modify it to meet your clients' specific needs. Why not customize it with your business name or your doctors'?

When precertification is necessary, be sure the doctor's office fills out a copy of the form and has it available when calling the carrier. If the carrier won't precertify a procedure over the phone, your client can fax or mail it with a cover letter. Or you can add this to the list of services you provide.

You'll want to be sure to get a copy of the completed precertification form with the preauthorization number filled in so that you can enter that number on the patient's claim form.

Not to worry. You'll find the procedure and diagnosis codes, otherwise known as the *CPT* (for *Current Procedural Terminology*) and *ICD-10* (for *International Classification of Diseases, 10th revision* and most properly called *ICD-10-CM*, for *Clinical Modification*) codes, on the superbill. Some MIBs prefer to set their doctors up with day sheets, a sort of running superbill list of each patient the doctor sees on a particular day (see page 45 for a sample day sheet).

Proper procedure codes are one of the most important parts of any insurance claim—they tell the carrier exactly what services or procedures were performed and/or what supplies were provided. Procedure coding can be extremely complex and in some cases has been elevated to the level of detailed craftsmanship. Hospitals and some large practices with in-house billers have employees who do nothing but

---

Fun with CPT Codes

CPT codes are divided into six sections, each of which specifies a different branch of medicine. Each section contains hundreds of different procedures.

Here's what they look like:

Anesthesiology	00100 to 01999
Surgery	10000 to 69999
Radiology, nuclear medicine, and diagnostic ultrasound	70000 to 79999
Pathology and laboratory	80000 to 89999
Medicine	90000 to 99199
Evaluation and management	99200 to 99499

The Evaluation and Management or E/M section is used to categorize types of visits by setting: office, hospital, home, clinic, nursing home, golf course, etc. These visits are further categorized by type of patient: new (one never before seen or one not seen in at least three years) or established, length of visit, complexity of visit, type of decision-making involved in the visit, the list goes on.

We won't run down every permutation here, but you should glance over these codes to get an idea of what exactly is involved so that when you see them on the superbill, you'll know what you're looking at. Take note, however, that all codes are subject to revisions. The only way to know exactly what is what is to make sure your coding books and software are up-to-date and to keep abreast of Medicare bulletins.

Precertification Form

Preauthorization number _____

Insurance carrier _____

Certification for admission _____ Surgery _____

Patient's name _____

Date of birth _____ Phone no. _____

Street address _____

City/state/zip _____

Subscriber's name _____

Address if different from patient's _____

_____

Member no. _____ Group no. _____

Admitting physician/surgeon _____

Provider no. _____

Hospital or facility _____

Planned admission/procedure date _____

Diagnosis/symptoms _____

Treatment/procedure _____

Estimated length of stay _____

Complicating factors _____

Second opinion required? _____ If yes, obtained? _____

Corroborating physician _____

Insurance carrier rep _____

Approval? _____

If no, reason for denial _____

coding. Coding requires a considerable knowledge of medical terminology, operative procedures, and other aspects of clinical medicine.

There are, for example, more than ten different codes to describe an office visit. Which code is used depends on whether the patient is new to the practice and also on the level of service provided. Think of it this way: A new patient requires more time than the old pal of the practice who's been seen twice a month for the past two years for the same medical problem. Dr. Whynot will want to spend time with New Patient Pamela, establishing a relationship, determining exactly what Pam's problem is, and working out a course of treatment. When Old Pal Peterson arrives in the office, however, Dr. Whynot can stick her head in, briefly inquire about any developments, and then leave the patient in the capable hands of her assistant for the routine treatment.

Think, too, of the differences between two types of emergency visits. There's every mother's nightmare, the head-wound-gushing-blood-that-needs-stitches, and then we have the handyman special, stepped-on-a-nail-in-the-garage-and-needs-a-tetanus-shot. In the first instance, Dr. Whynot needs to spend quite a bit of time with the patient, making sure there's no concussion involved and reviving fainting parents, in addition to suturing the wound. In the second instance, Handy Dan pops in, Dr. Whynot glances at his heel, determines that it's not infected, and bustles on to her next patient while her nurse stabs Dan with the tetanus needle.

You can see the time difference in these two types of visits. You can also see the difference in billable procedures. The first will involve a charge for an extended office visit, a charge for suturing the wound, and possibly another charge for a tetanus injection. There might also be a charge for tranquilizers for Mum. Handy Dan, on the other hand, will be charged for a brief office visit (or maybe none at all) and the injection.

The fees charged for the various office visits can be anywhere from $15 to $250, and insurance carriers—no dummies—are not going to pay $250 for the Handy Dan version. You can see why some MIBs feel so strongly that you should have a medical background before embarking on your business.

But again, don't panic. As a billing service, you are neither required—nor allowed—to provide or change a code for a medical procedure or office visit. That's the provider's job.

Most doctors specialize. Even good ol' GPs (general practitioners) specialize in basic illnesses—colds, the flu, conjunctivitis (pinkeye to you), simple lacerations, and sprained ankles. Anything out of their realm they send on to someone else. Other doctors do the same: Urologists refer to neurologists, cardiologists to oncologists. The point here is that each provider's superbill will consist of one page of procedures and diagnoses, each of which he's familiar with. As you work with his superbills, you'll become familiar with them as well.

Day Sheet

Day Sheet Page _____ of _____ Date _____ Day _____

	File #	Patient	Services	DX A/C	Charges	Payments	Balance Forward
1							
2							
3							
4							
5							
6							
7							
8							
9							
10							
11							
12							
13							
14							
15							
16							
17							
18							
19							
20							
21							
22							
23							
24							
25							
26							
27							
28							
29							
30							

Source: Health Care Management Services and Santiago SDS Inc.

Here is a day sheet. The column marked "DX A/C" can be translated as "diagnosis add or change" and is filled in when the patient is new to the practice or when his diagnosis changes. When a patient is first seen for a back strain, for example, the office staff fills in the correct ICD-10 code. On all successive visits for the same injury, the column is left blank. If the patient is subsequently treated for a new problem, the new code is filled in.

▲

Date: **8-2-0X**
Time Appt: **2:45**
Time Arrived: **2:45**
Patient: **Mischief, Kenny**

Wally Whatsit, M.D.
123 North South Street
Huckleberry, NH 00001
(000) 123-1234

\# _____
CHAMPUS # _____
NH LIC # _____
B.S. # _____

CPT	DESCRIPTION	FEE	CPT	DESCRIPTION	FEE	CPT	DESCRIPTION	FEE
	OFFICE VISITS			**LABORATORY: OTHER**		❑	Lesion Benign	
❑99201	NP One Problem Straight Forward	____	❑82150	Amylase Serum	____	❑11400	to .5 cm	____
❑99202	NP Expand Problem Straight Forward	____	❑86038	ANA	____	❑11401	.5 to 1.0 cm	____
❑99203	NP Detailed Low Complexity	____	❑85025	CBC w/Differential	____	❑11402	1.0 to 2.0 cm	____
❑99204	NP Comprehensive Hx Mod Hl Sever	____	❑80009	Coronary Risk	____	❑45330	Flexible Sigmoid	____
❑99205	NP Comp History High Complexity	____	❑82728	Ferritin	____	❑	Foreign Body Removal	
❑99211	Est. 5 Min. Minimal	____	❑86312	HIV	____	❑10121	Skin, Complex	____
❑99355	Comprehensive Exam	____	❑80059	Hepatitis Profile	____	❑10120	Skin, Simple	____
❑		____	❑86256	Lyme Titer	____	❑11740	Hematoma, Nail Puncture	____
	IMMUNIZATION/INJECTIONS		❑86403	Monospot	____	❑	Laceration	
❑95125	Allergy; Single Antigen	____	❑88150	Pap Smear	____	❑	Body/Neck/Scalp/Extremities	____
❑90782	B12 Estradiol Kenalog Testosterone	____	❑85610	Prothrombine Time	____	☑12001	Simple to 2.5 cm	**140.00**
❑90702	DT	____	❑86592	RPR/Syphilis	____	❑12002	Simple 2.5 to 7.5 cm	____
❑90731	Hepatitis B	____	❑80019	Chemistry Profile	____	❑12031	Intermed to 2.5 cm	____
❑90724	Influenza	____	❑84403	Testosterone	____	❑12032	Intermed 2.5 to 7.5 cm	____
❑86585	TB	____	❑84480	Thyroid Profile	____	❑	Hands/Feet/Neck	
❑90703	Tetanus	____	❑84443	TSH	____	❑12041	Intermed to 2.5 cm	____
❑		____	❑82205	Urine Drug	____	❑12042	Intermed 2.5 to 7.5 cm	____
	LABORATORY: IN OFFICE		❑		____	❑	Face/Mouth	
❑82948	Glucose	____	❑99000	HPSE Blood Draw	____	❑12011	Simple to 2.5 cm	____
❑86694	Herpes Simplex	____		**OFFICE PROCEDURES**		❑12013	Simple 2.5 to 5.0 cm	____
❑82270	Occult Blood	____	❑11100	Biopsy, Skin Lesion	____	❑12051	Intermed to 2.5 cm	____
❑81025	Pregnancy Test, Urine	____	❑69210	Cerumen Removal	____	❑12052	Intermed 2.5 to 5.0 cm	____
❑87060	Streptozyme-Throat/Nose	____	❑17340	Cryosurgery	____	❑15851	Suture Removal	____
❑		____	❑93000	EKG	____	❑		____

DIAGNOSIS

❑789.00	Abdominal Pain-(Unspecified sites)	❑558.9	Diarrhea	❑281.0	Pernicious Anemia		
❑789.06	Abdominal Pain-(Epigastric, Cramps)	❑780.4	Dizziness	❑462	Pharyngitis		
❑300.00	Acute Anxiety Reaction	❑780.7	Fatigue	❑V70.0	Physical Examination		
❑477.9	Allergic Rhinitis	❑610.1	Fibrocystic Breast Change	❑511.0	Pleurisy		
❑995.3	Allergy Reaction/Unspecified	❑535.5	Gastritis	❑486	Pneumonia		
❑285.9	Anemia	❑274.9	Gout	❑782.1	Rash		
❑413.9	Angina	❑V72.3	Gynecological Exam	❑788.0	Renal Colic		
❑716.90	Arthritis	❑784.0	Headache	❑473.9	Sinusitis		
❑429.2	ASCVD	❑455.3	Hemorrhoids/External	❑308.9	Situational Disorder		
❑414.00	ASHD	❑553.3	Hiatal Hernia	❑V58.3	Suture Removal		
❑493.90	Asthmatic Bronchitis	❑401.9	Hypertension	❑726.90	Tendonitis		
❑427.31	Atrial Fibrillation	❑380.4	Impacted Cerumen	❑257.2	Testicular Hormone Deficiency		
❑724.2	Back Pain/Lumbalgia	❑684	Impetigo	❑435.9	TIA		
❑847.9	Back Sprain/Strain	❑847.1	Influenza	❑463	Tonsilitis		
❑611.72	Breast Lump	❑564.1	Irritable Bowel Syndrome	❑465.9	URI		
❑490	Bronchitis	❑386.3	Labyrinthitis	❑599.0	UTI		
❑682.9	Cellulitis	❑627.2	Menopausal Symptoms	❑616.10	Vaginitis		
❑786.52	Chest Pain	❑346.0	Migraine	❑787.03	Vomiting		
❑428.0	Congestive Heart Failure	❑787.02	Nausea	❑V20.2	Well Child Care		
❑786.2	Cough	❑278.0	Obesity	❑V65.40	Counseling Health		
❑311	Depression	❑380.1	Otitis Externa	☑187.0	**Head Laceration**		
❑250.00	Diabetes	❑382.9	Otitis Media	❑			

Previous Balance	Today's Charges	Total Due	Today's Payment	Balance	If not better, return or phone
			$140.00		PRN ____ Weeks ____ Months ____ Units ____
					Next Appointment Date:
					Doctor's Signature: **Wally Whatsit**

Here is a superbill. Notice how it neatly condenses the diagnosis, service performed, and fee charged into one tidy package.

Incidentally, you might find it interesting—and sobering—to know that the National Center for Health Statistics recently approved 11 new codes to indicate a terrorist threat. These codes became effective Oct. 1, 2002.

Verify and Clarify

The more you know about coding, the more help you can be to your doctors—and to yourself. It goes without saying that the more money you make for the doctor, the more you make for yourself.

> **Smart Tip** Tip...
>
> Tipping off your doctors to new coding techniques is a darn good marketing technique. It shows them that you are actively increasing their revenues in ways they might not have discovered for themselves. Remember, you have the secret decoder ring!

You can't legally take your trusty red pen, cross out the doctor's codes, and substitute those you think are more interesting. You can, however, guide your providers toward in-the-know billing techniques.

The San Diego MIB says that when she finds incorrect codes on her clients' day sheets, she shoots them off a quick fax clarifying what the code should actually read. "I'm assisting with the coding, but I'm technically not the coder. But I know what the basics are and what should be there and what shouldn't be there, so what I do is just verify and clarify with the office."

"It's not a matter of just entering the numbers that are on the sheet," the Denver MIB explains. "What I find with my physicians is that they know what they've done—they just don't know how to express it on a superbill. Because I can say to my doctor, 'OK, you did this procedure. Did you do a follow-up telephone call on it? Did you know you can combine that with your next visit and you can get paid for that?'

> **Beware!**
>
> Be certain that what you're doing is updating your doctors to the latest techniques, not telling them how to code. This is their territory and their responsibility. Make sure you keep all superbills, day sheets, or other materials to back up that what you've entered on a claim came from the provider's hand.

And the doctors [respond], 'I can?'

"Actually, when I get a new doctor I do a superbill evaluation for them so that I can see what kind of codes they're using and which codes are no longer in use. Then I just give them tidbits now and then from seminars that I attend, let them know that 'Gee, I learned you can do this,' or 'I learned something about this procedure code.'"

She tries to do some revamping of the superbills each provider has been using. Most have reprinted their superbills based on what they've learned from her. But her doctor training doesn't stop there.

Don't Fool with Fraud

The National Health Care Anti-Fraud Association reports a loss of three percent of total health-care costs to fraud, which amounts to about $51 billion dollars per year. Some groups even estimate the cost to be higher at around 10 percent, or $170 billion. To counteract this staggering sum, HCFA has teamed up with the FBI and other investigative agencies to seek out and destroy fraudulent providers. According to a recent report from HGS Administrators, a Medicare carrier with facilities in Delaware, New Jersey, Pennsylvania, and Virginia, fraudulent acts include these types of creative exercises:

- ○ Billing for services or supplies that were not performed, provided, or requested
- ○ Billing for noncovered services as if they were covered
- ○ Misrepresenting diagnoses
- ○ Sending in false claims
- ○ Paying fees for patient referrals
- ○ Altering claim forms and records

"Make sure that you are really specific about this code for me," she says in illustration of how she instructs her doctors. "I just pass on different things to them, such as modifiers and when they can use them and when to let me know that they've done something that I can tack a modifier on and get them more money—or get them paid in the first place."

Beware!

Remember that CPT codes are revised annually. Don't skip a year. If you do, you could provide yourself with hours of awful torture trying to determine which changes made during the previous year apply to your clients' superbills.

In the Groove

The CPT codes are revised every year, which means you need to stay up-to-date. When you take on a new client, you should—like the Denver MIB—grade his or her current superbill. Does it contain the latest codes? If not, recommend changes. You're asking for trouble if you use outdated codes. The chances are great that the carrier won't pay the same on an old code; in fact, it may refuse to recognize it. Either way, reimbursement won't be swift, and you won't look good.

Leveling the CPT Codes

Unraveling the mysteries of procedure codes can seem as daunting as trying to decode a World War I secret spy message. But if you think they're baffling now, be glad you weren't starting out any time before 1983, when Medicare and HCFA developed the current system. During those Dark Ages of medical coding, there were more than 120 different coding systems floating around the United States.

The current system is the brainchild of the American Medical Association, which updates it each year, and is divided into three levels, sort of like the consecutively deeper levels of a top-secret underground military installation. The entire package is called the *HCFA Common Procedure Coding System*, or *HCPCS*, which those in the know pronounce Hick-Pix.

The top level—the one used most often—is called the *CPT-4* (for *Current Procedural Terminology*) and contains more than 7,000 codes that are updated yearly. These are the codes that describe the doctor's services, procedures, and visits.

Level II comes next. Level II codes are concerned with durable medical equipment, medical supplies such as gauze and syringes, chemotherapy, and a host of miscellaneous services.

The bottom level and—to follow our secret underground facility analogy—therefore the most obscure, is *HCPCS Local Level III*. These codes are used on a local level by Medicare offices in different states to describe new procedures that only they might recognize.

But let's not look on the grim side. Let's say you review your new client's codes and suggest changes. Right away, you've presented yourself as someone knowledgeable in her field. You send in claims with up-to-date codes. The doctor—who obviously didn't even realize he was working with outmoded material—is reimbursed in record time. You're a savior!

This might be another point where you've gotten up to refill your coffee mug, come back and muttered, "Did I miss something while I was interfacing with Mr. Coffee? Just how do I get in the groove on all this up-to-date CPT stuff?"

Well, you haven't missed a beat. There are many ways to scope out coding scoops. One way, as the Denver MIB suggests, is to attend coding seminars. Another is to take training provided by reputable medical billing business opportunity vendors. Yet another is to subscribe to—and read—newsletters and bulletins.

Most Medicare and Medicaid carriers provide free seminars explaining how their programs work and supplying valuable billing information. This is an excellent way

▲

to increase your knowledge and keep up with the ever-changing requirements. Some organizations will put you on their mailing lists and notify you of classes. Others place only doctors' offices on their lists. In this case, you should try to cultivate a friendship with an office manager and see if you can coast in as a member of her staff. There's no cost, and it's well worth the effort.

Other coding resources are available by surfing the internet. America Online has MIB forums where you can either "lurk," reading other people's questions and answers without participating (recommended for the strong, silent—or shy—type), or participate actively, tossing out coding questions to your fellow billers. You'll be amazed at what you can learn in these places. You can subscribe to listservs (online groups) for chiropractors, for example. You can surf government, lobbyist, and corporate-type web sites—HCFA, the AMA, Blue Cross-Blue Shield—and pick up information.

Not nearly as exhilarating, but a lot more time-efficient, is yet another source: medical coding books. Ingenix, a mail order house specializing in medical coding books, will happily send you books, spiral binders, software, and even cheat sheets on everything you could ever want to know about coding. (Their mailing address, phone number, and web site address, as well as those of other excellent medical text houses, are listed in Appendix A.)

OK, that about wraps it up for CPT codes. But there's more on the secret decoder front. We still have to discuss diagnoses. After all, what's the point in having a procedure code if you don't have a diagnosis to be treated?

The Diagnosis Code Dirt

Diagnosis or ICD-10 codes are developed by the WHO (the World Health Organization, not the rock group). These codes are used internationally to describe accidents, illnesses, and injuries for the purposes of medical research and reporting. This, of course, includes reporting diagnoses to insurance carriers to support the procedure code charge.

Here we hark back to our example of the gushing-blood head injury. The diagnosis here would most likely be 187.0, *Laceration of the Head*, for the child, who was probably happily slurping a Tootsie Pop five minutes after being sutured, and *Acute Anxiety Reaction* or *Congestive Heart Failure* for the mother. Now, if you look at the bottom portion of the superbill on page 46, you'll see a nice checkmark in the "Diagnosis" section, right next to 187.0. If you skim around, you'll also note *Acute Anxiety Reaction* listed as 300.00 and *Congestive Heart Failure* shown as 428.0.

The zeros after the decimal point are referred to as the *modifier* and (surprise!) are used to modify the basic code. If we really wanted to give poor Mum a heart attack, for example, which we most certainly would *not*, we could bill for a *Fracture at the Base of the Skull*, which is an 801 code. We could modify this code by adding a .1, which would also indicate a *Closed Fracture with Cerebral Laceration and Contusion*. If we added a .2, we'd be indicating a diagnosis of *Closed Fracture of the Skull with Subarachnoid, Subdural, and Extradural Hemmorhage*.

But let's not do this to our little patient—or to Mum. Let's switch it back to a simple childhood cut, the kind that look far worse than they actually are, the kind some children actually sport as a sort of after-the-fact red badge of courage.

Now, we have our ICD-10 code of 187.0. If you glance back at the top half of the superbill in the CPT code section, you will see a nice checkmark next to 12001, which is the office procedure for suturing a *Laceration, Body/Neck/Scalp/Extremities, Simple to 2.5 cm*. See, simple!

You'll also see the doctor's fee scribbled beside the CPT code and the total dashed along the bottom of the superbill. At the top are the patient's name and the date of the appointment. Now you have everything you need to enter the bill into your computer program.

The Denied ICD-10 Code

If a claim is denied because of the diagnosis code, it's usually for one of the following reasons:

- No diagnosis is provided.
- The diagnosis given is inconsistent with the service or procedure provided.
- The diagnosis doesn't substantiate the need or level of service provided.
- Multiple diagnoses are given, which confuses the claims examiner.

OK! The first two problems are easy to solve. Make sure you have at least one diagnosis for each procedure or group of related procedures, and be sure the diagnosis is consistent with the procedure listed. The insurance company isn't going to pay for a Pap smear when the diagnosis is male pattern baldness.

Moving on to Problem Number 3: If the diagnosis doesn't validate the level of service, then the doctor has probably failed to code for extenuating circumstances. Let's say, for example, that Dr. Whosit billed a two-hour procedure at a three-hour rate. Insurance carriers love to deny claims, and this gives them the perfect opportunity. To get Dr. Whosit paid, you'll need to send an explanation with the charge, making it clear that the procedure took extra time because the patient's diabetes complicated the surgery, or because the patient had an alien like Sigourney Weaver's wedged in his intestines.

Problem Number 4 can also be solved with some vigilance on your part. Many doctors have a tendency to over-diagnose for the purposes of insurance billing, using two, three, or even four different ICD-10 codes to justify a single procedure. In this case, more is not better. All this does is create confusion in the mind of the claims examiner, who will then try to decide which, if any, of the multiple codes submitted justify the procedure—and its payment. Often such claims are either sent back to

▲

Tip...

Smart Tip

Even though she uses a courier service, the California MIB spends a lot of time visiting clients. When you do this—picking up materials or "just checking in"—you develop a rapport with your doctors and their staff. You're accessible. You can problem-solve while the problems are small instead of large.

the doctor for additional information or forwarded to a nurse or physician reviewer.

The rule here is the same one that applies to Army details or IRS audits: Don't volunteer. Don't give them any more to think about than is necessary.

Just the Fax, Ma'am

Now that you know all about coding, let's backtrack a bit. How are you going to get the superbills or day sheets to take your CPT and ICD-10 codes from?

Most MIBs rely on one or a combination of three methods: the fax machine, personal pickup and delivery, and the USPS. When you make your decision, keep in mind that you'll be dealing with more than just superbills—you'll also have patient information sheets, explanation of benefits (EOBs) from insurance carriers, and correspondence from patients and insurers.

The New Jersey MIB receives her material via fax. "Every once in a while, I'll make a pickup if I'm in the area or if they have an overflow," she says. She cut down on the amount of paper coming through her machine by redesigning her clients' superbills (which, she confesses, "I despise") into day sheets. "If you have 20 patients that day, instead of 20 superbills, I've got one day sheet with all 20 patients and all the information on it."

She compiles each day's faxes and then sorts them into baskets hung on her office wall, one for each client. Since she's also sorted them in chronological order, she can process them by date received. "This way, I always have a backup to see why I processed this first," she says, adding, "but that's never been a problem."

Faxing can be viewed as the best way to go: Information can be sent quickly without worrying about weighing, stamping, or delivery time. But it can also be perceived as a techno-pain. Either machine can jam midtransmission; either machine can experience a line error that breaks the connection midtransmission; your machine can run out of paper midstream. Both you and your client should have a dedicated line so lengthy fax sessions don't tie up your telephone.

The San Diego MIB decided to go with the USPS and provided her doctor with the first quarter's priority mail envelopes and stamps. His staff simply pops a week's worth of day sheets into one of these envelopes, along with any other necessary materials, and consigns it to the postal service.

The personal pickup option works best for the Virginia teacher/MIB. "I'm involved with after-school activities," Kim H. explains, "so I set [aside] Wednesday of

Card 'Em, Dan-o

Patients change and lose jobs, spouses, and dependents with sometimes amazing rapidity. Some patients can change surnames several times in the course of as many years. Any of these alterations can result in a loss of or substantial change in insurance coverage.

Therefore, make sure your clients do the following:

○ *Card 'em.* Ask to see insurance identification cards for all new patients. Many cards contain valuable information such as special telephone numbers or even an explanation of basic coverage in addition to patient ID.

○ *Copy it.* Make a photocopy of the card and use it to verify the member number and/or group number on the "Patient Registration" form. Insurance ID cards usually carry the effective date of coverage. It's important to note that these cards are frequently issued and distributed to beneficiaries in advance—sometimes as much as 30 days in advance—of the effective date. If the provider renders service prior to the effective date on the card, the patient, not the provider, is responsible for the fee.

○ *Ask for it.* Obtain job information, including length of employment. Most group plans have a waiting period of at least 30 days and frequently 60 to 90 days before an employee is eligible for coverage.

○ *Update it.* Unless a doctor is seeing a patient with unusual frequency, the patient should always be asked if there have been any changes in address, phone number, employment, or insurance coverage since the last visit.

○ *Check it.* Ask Medicaid patients for current proof of eligibility whenever they seek medical care. They are required by federal law to provide it. Eligibility in these programs changes frequently, and benefits will not be paid without adequate proof of eligibility at the time of treatment.

every week and I go by each office and pick things up. Then if they have any questions, we take care of it there."

The Walnut Creek MIB also employs the personal pickup option but with a twist. Her beat is the entire San Francisco Bay area, so she uses a courier service. The service picks up from and delivers to her clients' offices every day, five days a week.

In Rockford, Illinois, the former pastor used to drop by his clients' offices once or twice a week, depending on the size of the practice. But now he does everything virtually—either via fax or e-mail.

Organically Organized

Whatever methods you choose, the materials you'll be working with will fall into these basic categories:

- New patient information sheets and information sheets detailing changes to established patients' files
- Superbills or day sheets with CPT and ICD-10 codes written in or checked off
- EOBs for previously submitted claims
- Mail from insurance carriers and from patients regarding previously submitted claims or changes in policies or patient information

Ideally, all these materials will be presorted for you in chronological order and batched by type of material. You may want to train your clients to present them to you this way, or you may prefer to save them the hassle and sort through it yourself.

If you pick up the material in person, you should take the time to give everything the once-over and make sure you have the information you need. Look, for example, at the superbills or day sheets. Are codes entered or checked? Is the necessary patient information entered and legible? Is it clear whom mail is from or about? Giving all this a glance in your client's office can save you time—you can collect missing information then instead of having to call the client when you return to your office.

If you're an organically organized person, this extra step in the client's office will be easy for you. If you're easily distracted or flustered, you may find this difficult at first. But take a deep breath, take it easy and train yourself to look things over. Realize that the impression you leave will be one of quiet efficiency.

Once you get back to your own space—or once you receive the material from your friendly mail carrier or fax machine—you'll want to sort through and organize it as we've discussed.

The San Diego MIB/former nurse, who receives her day sheets by mail, makes a habit of faxing requests for corrected coding to her doctor. "They would rather you ask a lot of questions than just decide on your own what you think should happen," she says.

If she feels any information is missing, she dashes off a fax request, giving the client the option of calling or faxing back the response. "I do that," she explains, "because I don't want too many verbal requests over the phone, so

Beware!

Newbie MIBs are sometimes confused about whether they can accept reimbursement checks for the doctor in their company name. The answer is no. Medicare's reassignment laws stipulate that payment must go to the physician, unless he reassigns payment to the facility—an HMO, for example—where he works on-site. As a full-practice management company, you can, however, have checks in the doctor's name come to your office for deposit into his account.

that I have something to back up that I have requested [the material]."

The Instant "A"

Your software miraculously produces your claims, ready for online delivery, but to where? This is where the clearing-house comes in. Like a railroad round-house sending steaming locomotives to all corners of the country from its central location, the clearinghouse rounds up all your claims and routes them to the proper insurance carriers.

As an added bonus, it reconfigures your data into whatever format each carrier requires, a nice touch because, although the HCFA 1500 is the industry standard, insurers still insist on variations on the main theme.

Even better, the clearinghouse automatically *audits* each claim, checking it for clerical errors and omissions before sending it on to the carrier. When it finds a goof,

The Eligibility Factor

During predetermination, the doctor finds out from the insurance carrier the maximum dollar amount it will pay for certain services, procedures, or supplies before he goes ahead and provides them. This is somewhat akin to the good old days when you stood around in the department store while they called your charge card to make sure you had enough balance remaining to cover that gorgeous sequined gown.

Predetermination (also known as coverage or benefits verification) lets both the doctor and the patient know how much of the doctor's charge will be reimbursed by the carrier. It also allows both doctor and patient to make arrangements to cover any difference between the actual charge amount and the allowed amount before service is rendered.

The doctor's office calls the insurance carrier at the phone number listed on the back of the patient's insurance card and explains that they want to verify eligibility. They should then ask the carrier a series of questions, which you can find on the "Predetermination Form," on page 56.

You can give copies of this form to your clients as is or customize it with your business name or your client's. Like the "Precertification Form," this is a great marketing/public relations piece.

Predetermination Form

Patient's name _____

Date of birth _____

Subscriber's name _____

Member no. _____ Group no. _____

Insurance carrier _____

Phone no. _____

❑ Is there a deductible? _____

❑ If yes, what is it? _____

❑ Has the deductible been met? _____

❑ Is a portion of the intended fee covered under major medical benefits? _____

❑ Is a portion covered under basic benefits? _____

❑ What are the benefits for inpatient care? _____

_____

❑ What are the benefits for outpatient or office care? _____

_____

❑ What percentage of the charge do you reimburse? _____

❑ Is that a percentage of the fee or of usual and customary reimbursement (UCR)? ____

❑ If UCR, can you give me a rough estimate of your reimbursement for our charge of

$_____ for a _____ (code)? $_____

❑ Is there an annual maximum? _____

❑ If yes, how much has been used? _____

it redirects the claim back to you so you can correct the problem. This way you get an instant "A" with the carrier.

All this may sound alarmingly high-tech, but it's not. If you're the least bit main-streamed into today's world, you've been using *electronic data interchange*, or EDI, for years. Every time you snatch some cash from the ATM or pass your credit card through the little scanner at the supermarket, you're initiating an EDI transaction.

You may, however, choose not to use a clearinghouse for all your claims. In most areas it's just as easy—and less expensive—to submit directly to Medicare and Blue Cross as it is to send claims through the clearinghouse.

Clearinghouses generally charge a processing fee, which ranges from 35 cents to 95 cents per claim. Some charge an annual registration or membership fee of up to $300; others add a one-time fee of up to $50 per doctor. (We'll go over all this in depth in Chapter 6.)

The Old-Fashioned Way

Electronic claims transmission is the wave of the future, but not everyone is on a surfing safari yet. Some insurers still accept only paper claims, and some MIBs prefer dealing with paper claims.

"We do not do electronic filing of claims," says the Denver MIB, "as we've had very bad luck finding a clearinghouse that would efficiently handle physicians' claims and do it correctly."

New clients are surprised when she tells them she does only paper claims, especially since the other billing services in her area all file electronically, but she manages to reassure them. "I get payment back within two to three weeks on most all my claims," she asserts, "even though I send them through the U.S. Postal Service."

Another joy of running your own billing service: You can use any system that works for you.

Submission Time

After you've entered the day's claims, it's time for the big moment—submitting them. If you're working with paper claims, you print them out—one copy for your files and one for the insurer—and set your copy aside. Then it's just a matter of fold, lick, and stamp.

If you're working with electronic claims, you'll go to the online portion of your software and send the day's batch speeding to your clearinghouse or carrier. Some clearinghouses will *drop the claims to paper* for you, meaning you send the claim online and the clearinghouse prints a paper copy and sends it on its merry way.

By the time you've scooted to the kitchen for a fresh cup of coffee, the clearing-house will have received your claims, forwarded the good, or clean, copies to the respective carriers, and alerted you to the rejected ones—if any—via a report called the *Audit/Error Report* or *Sender Log*.

At this point you can and should print the report for your records. You can also make corrections to the rejects and resubmit. In the case of rejects (such as incorrect codes) that need doctor clarification, you can call the client immediately or set the claim aside to be dealt with later.

Playing the Insurance Game

A given in the medical billing industry is that insurers will thwart you at every turn with an apparently insatiable desire to deny claims. They seem to find every possible reason to reject a claim or to avoid prompt payment. The savvy MIB takes on the challenge instead of being oppressed by it.

"You learn how to play with the insurance companies," counsels Mary V., the Maryland MIB. "We have to view it as a game. I look at it as somebody's got to win. And I don't like to lose."

Mary advises not taking the game personally and offers the fact that, with her philosophy, she doesn't get a lot of rejections. "Because if you learn the game," she says, "if you learn what they're looking for, then they'll pay."

As an example, Mary cites an HMO that rejects a paper claim because the referral wasn't attached, even though it was fastened with three staples. "You just send it back in as quickly as possible," she says. She speeds the EOB or denial back through with not only a copy of the referral attached but the referral number, the date and her initials inked on the front. "And they don't reject that one."

Mary cheerfully explains that it's also possible to intimidate the insurance carrier. "You do it nicely," she says. "But they know that you're not going to give up. It's basically if they know you're serious about what you're talking about—you're going to call them back—then they will go on and pay it."

The Walnut Creek, California, MIB also cites HMOs as difficult adversaries. "Trying to get timely payments is sometimes very difficult even if you electronically bill," she says. "They know all of the ways not to pay you. They will send our patient, for instance, a letter requesting further information, and the patient presumes the billing is being handled and frequently ignores their letter, so they don't have to respond until the patient responds. So it's a cat-and-mouse game."

The New Jersey MIB, who used to sit on the insurer side of the fence, adds with a touch of whimsy, "I used to fight on behalf of the insurance companies, and now I fight with them."

The Rejected Claim

Face it. No matter how brilliant you are, you're going to have some rejected claims. Sometimes it's because the insurance company is playing fast and loose; sometimes it's because somebody left out vital information.

The following are common reasons for rejected claims:

- ○ Missing or incomplete diagnosis
- ○ Missing or incorrect subscriber and/or group number
- ○ Diagnosis does not correspond with or support the services or procedures performed
- ○ Diagnosis is not ICD-10 coded
- ○ Reasons for multiple visits made the same day are not given
- ○ Charges are not itemized
- ○ Fee column is left blank
- ○ Required information about prescription drugs or durable medical equipment is not included
- ○ Missing or incorrect CPT codes
- ○ Patient did not answer all questions on his portion of form
- ○ Incorrect dates—for example, surgery shown taking place before pre-op exam, or discharge date preceding admission date
- ○ Missing dates
- ○ Illegible claim—smeary, smudged, handwritten in a scrawl, coffee-spill blurred
- ○ Service or procedure not covered by policy

In Illinois, Curt J. has experienced the biller/carrier relationship quite differently. "Actually," he says, "that part of [the gamesmanship] surprised me. Most of the time it's really straightforward. It's either an error, a glitch, or a communication problem. Sometimes it can take a little bit to figure out, but once it's figured out, it's done. There's actually very few of the games that you hear insurance companies play."

Back in Virginia, Kim H., the teacher, finds that interactions with insurers don't always go quite so smoothly. When she sees a denial on an EOB, she reaches for the phone and calls the carrier. "You wouldn't believe that you could be on hold for 10 minutes just to check out one claim," she says ruefully. "When I get through, they tell me what the problem is, so I immediately try to take care of it. And then I just rebill it."

Since she's in school until midafternoon, her time is at a premium. "It's hard," Kim admits. "A lot of times if I have quite a few [denials], I'll take the planning period that I have at school, which is about 45 minutes, and I'll call during that time. A lot of times I have to come straight home and then from 3:30 to 5:00 I try to call."

Smart Tip   Tip...

Most insurers have an 800 number. Be sure you use it, so your on-hold time is on their quarter instead of yours. If the phone number you have is not toll free, ask for one when you get a live being on the line; frequently, they'll give you one for future reference. (Or hang up and call back on the 800 number.)

Winning the Game

It should be obvious by now that to be a savvy MIB, you have to be willing to play, and play to win. You can't be a wimp.

If you have not received payment on a paper claim within 45 days after submission, it's time to find out what the problem is.

Sometimes it's a simply a matter of nonreceipt. The claim may have been lost in the mail, sucked into an alternate universe or mysteriously vaporized within the carrier's computer system.

Some carriers require written inquiries; some Medicare and Medicaid carriers require specific inquiry forms; some carriers allow telephone inquiries. In any case, you should copy all written inquiries and annotate them to the patient file. For telephone questions, be sure to get the name and phone extension of the person you speak with and note these details on your file along with the date and particulars of the conversation. If it's apparent the payer has made an error on a claim, don't hesitate to challenge the payment amount. Medicare and other insurers will correct mistakes if you bring them to their attention. Even if you made the error, it's always possible to resubmit a claim.

When you discover an error on a claim that has resulted in insufficient reimbursement, submit a corrected claim. Clearly mark the claim: *Corrected Billing—Not a Duplicate Claim*. Add a note specifying the error and, if necessary, additional documentation to support your correction.

Don't think your entire MIB life will be spent battling insurers. Most of the claims you submit will be paid quickly, allowing you to post the payment to the patient's account and bill the patient for any co-payment due.

When you do encounter the odd problem claim, however, you'll be armed and ready. You already know the secret: Be prepared to fix and/or fight.

When you receive a patient's EOB (explanation of benefits, remember?), start grading the insurer's work. Compare the charge amount listed with the charge amount in your patient's account ledger.

Check your client's codes against those on the EOB for errors or changes that the carrier might have made. Sometimes payers will down-code a procedure from the actual one to a less costly one—inadvertently or intentionally—and pay based on the substituted code. In some cases, the payer's data entry department may simply have transposed two digits in a CPT code, resulting in a different procedure from the one performed. In other cases, your client might have used an outdated CPT code that

Faster than a Speeding Bullet

As a mega-MIB, your goal is to get claims paid as quickly as possible. You can't leap tall buildings in a single bound (at least we don't think you can), but you can get claims reimbursed at seemingly superspeeds. Try these tips for starters:

○ *Rank procedures by order of charge amount.* When entering charges from the superbill or day sheet, be sure to enter all procedures performed on the same date in order, from the most expensive to the least expensive. Insurers will reduce the values of all procedures listed after the primary one. If you list the procedures as suggested, however, your claim will result in the highest possible reimbursement in light of the carrier's reduction of values. You should always list the full charge for each procedure and let the carrier reduce them—don't help them out. In most cases, the first procedure is considered at 100 percent of its value, the second at 75 percent, the third at 50 percent and the fourth at 25 percent.

○ *Don't send documentation unless asked.* Although electronic claims don't require documentation, people tend to send documentation along with paper claims. Don't. Unless the provider is using a CPT code for an unlisted procedure or explaining unusual circumstances (unsticking a patient's eyelids after a superglue accident, for example), you should not send operative reports or other documentation. Most procedures are fairly common, so carriers won't even be interested in the details. If they want supporting information, they'll ask. Otherwise, let sleeping insurers lie.

○ *Send even hospital bills frequently.* Even for hospitalized patients, carriers prefer to get frequent, small claims instead of one huge claim following the patient's discharge. While some providers hold hospital charges as a consideration to the hospitalized patient, you can help avoid a tragic relapse caused by a mammoth doctor's fee simply by doing your billing as you—and the patient's care—go along. Also, holding claims through a long hospitalization is risky. You could discover that by the time you get around to filing your claim, the patient's benefits have already been exhausted.

Smart Tip

Tip...

If you're not getting a response from a recalcitrant carrier, use your patient as a collection tool. Inform him of the problem and let him go toe-to-toe with the insurer. In many cases, this will result in a quick resolution of the problem.

the insurer did not—or refused to—recognize. Here the insurer may review the claim and pop in the valid code for you or deny the claim and leave it up to you to resubmit.

Time Juggling

Except for having to work within the time constraints of the carriers' office hours when dealing with problem claims, you can structure your day any way that fits your lifestyle.

"I just work into the evening if I need to have the extra time," says a Montana MIB. As a grandmom rather than young mom, she has the luxury of time. "I'll just juggle my time, and I don't have to worry that I have an 8-to-5 job. I can do the work that needs to be completed in my time frame."

The San Diego biller has her hands full with an 11-year-old son and 7-year-old daughter. Before the kids are up and about, she checks her e-mail for new information from fellow MIBs, then pulls up her prospect software to see who she has scheduled to contact that day. In between getting her chicks fed, dressed, and off to school, she compiles lists: which insurance companies need to be called, what missing items need to be faxed to her client.

To avoid the unprofessional sound of children squealing in the background, she makes all her phone calls in the morning while the kids are at school. She schedules errands between noon and 2 P.M. when most medical offices are closed so she doesn't miss business calls. In the afternoons, she does her data entry, pulls up reports, balances her accounts, and checks through new material, and of course, answers the phone.

"Then," the former nurse says, "I sort of semi-prepare myself for the next day. By the end of the day, I back up my database for my client. And then every week, I'll do a system backup."

Lest you think you could never keep up her pace, she adds, "I'm still in the learning stages. I'm constantly adapting to what I'm doing, and sometimes I worry that I spend too much time on something. But it's all a learning process."

The New Jersey MIB, who also has two young children, usually processes her claims from 12:30 to 4:00 P.M. while the kids are stashed away at school. After supper, she goes back to her computer and hits the keyboard again. She schedules two days a week, generally Thursday and Friday, for follow-up work. "That's for any problems that come up with the clients," she says, "if I have to call the insurance company, do an appeal, things like that."

And that's not all. "I'm often working Saturdays," she says. "I refuse to work on Sunday, though. No matter what."

Diagnosing Your Market

Every business needs consumers for its products or services to, as the Vulcans so eloquently put it, live long and prosper. Now that you know what running a medical billing service entails, you need to diagnose, or target, your market to determine who your potential clients will be, what geographic area you'll draw from, and what specific services you'll offer to lure them in.

This is an important phase in the mega-MIB building project. The proper market research can help boost your billing service into a true profit center, and the more research you do, the better prepared you'll be before you officially open your doors, the less floundering you are likely to do. This chapter, therefore, homes in on market research tips and techniques for the budding medical billing service. First up:

Tripping Doctors

Your target market—the clients you are aiming for—can be as wide as the field of modern medicine. Any health-care provider is fair game. You can go after family practitioners, providers of every specialty from geriatrics to pediatrics, chiropractors and osteopaths, obstetricians and oncologists, proctologists and podiatrists. You can target mental health professionals, psychiatrists, and psychologists. And don't forget the groups of providers not normally associated with doctoring, such as dentists, social workers, nursing homes, ambulance services, pharmacists, home health practitioners, providers of durable medical equipment, and providers of bionic body parts. The only essential requirement is that they bill or receive reimbursement from insurance carriers or patients.

On a Mission

The mission statement is an important part of brainstorming any new business. This is where you state your company's intent or goals and what you'll do to achieve them. You might choose something like:

Acme Billing Service will provide full-practice management to neurologists and urologists, offering quality billing, patient accounting, and tips and updates on the latest collection techniques. Through the speed and efficiency of our collections, we will become recognized as the premier neurology and urology billing service in Huckleberry, New Hampshire. We will have a ten-physician base within two years.

Here's another example:

Zephyr Claims Services will provide the best and brightest in claims billing for nursing homes and hospices. Because of our expertise with Medicare and our ability to get claims reimbursed quickly, we will sign five clients in our first year of operation and will have 20 by the end of our second year.

Like everything else we've covered in this chapter, what you choose to say and how you say it is up to you. Your mission statement is as unique and personal as you are.

Mission Statement Worksheet

Fill in your mission statement on this worksheet. Remember that the mission statement should clearly define the following:

○ *A view to the future.* How do you envision your business down the road, in one year, two years, ten years?

○ *A view to your clients' perception of your company.* How do you want them to think of you?

○ *A view to the medical community at large.* How do you wish the medical community to perceive your company?

Mission Statement for

_____

(your business name)

_____

_____

_____

_____

_____

This doesn't mean, however, that your best technique is to stand at the hospital doors, tripping doctors as they walk by. Targeting by definition means homing in on a particular group.

If you have had previous experience working in a particular medical specialty, for example, you might want to target that market first. You'll feel comfortable with the jargon and procedures so your sales pitch—and your initial billings—will go smoother and easier. As an added bonus, you may already have contacts in the field who can either become your first clients or steer you on to colleagues in the field.

If you're a newbie in the world of medicine, you might want to start off targeting doctors in a single specialty, such as psychiatrists, chiropractors, cardiologists, or dentists. These providers' practices involve a narrower range of diagnoses and procedures than a family practitioner, general surgeon or internist, so you'll have fewer new codes tossed in your lap at the get-go.

This is a good, starting-from-scratch strategy, but don't let it dictate or limit your contacts. Most MIBs find that the first client they land, through whatever means, is the specialty they end up going with.

Curt J.'s client base originally consisted of one dentist and two chiropractors. The dentist was easy—he's a personal friend. Of the chiropractors, the first was a case of serendipity.

"I ran across a struggling chiropractic office," the Illinois MIB relates. "They just needed help, so I began to help them. Shortly after we began building a relationship, they filed for bankruptcy. But it was enough of a foot in the door that they had a couple of friends that they recommended to me, and that helped me land a couple of accounts."

The New Jersey MIB's clients are all mental health professionals. Of 26 individual providers, every one is a psychiatrist, psychologist, or biofeedback technician. Surprisingly, however, she did not actively go after the mental health field. "It just sort of found me," she says. "Once I got my first client—who was actually given to me—it rolled from there by word of mouth and referrals."

The nub of these experiences—that the first client helps to land others—is a familiar one. We heard over and over from just about everyone we have spoken with in the MIB trade that doctors talk. When one likes what you are doing, he will tell another and she will tell another. Next thing you know, you will be knee-deep in doctors.

"Just by default, my first client was a neurologist," the Denver MIB says. "I haven't really marketed my services; it's been by word of mouth." Her stable of clients is 14 strong—13 neurologists and one family physician. "That's not by choice; it just happened that way. I guess my name has been passed around in the neurology locker room."

Mary V. originally specialized in neurology as well as oncology. She felt she was better off sticking to the fields she enjoys, ones in which she is familiar with the coding. She's also wisely figured that by specializing, she'll be less affected by regulatory changes than if they had a broader client base. "When something happens with one specialty," Mary explains, "then it would happen for all of [the doctors] as far as changes in any rule or code or something like that. It is just much quicker, much easier to follow up on. My staff and I don't have to be experts in everything."

Fun Fact

There were 884,974 physicians in the United States in 2004, according to the American Medical Association. In case that doesn't give you a big enough pool to plumb, take heart: Another 17,382 people were accepted to U.S. medical schools the same year.

Does Size Really Matter?

OK, you've decided—or you are thinking about planning on deciding—which areas to specialize in. Good! But you are far from laying your decision-making skills to rest. Next, you have to think about what size practices you will want to focus on. Any size is fine, of course, but you might consider starting off with small to midsized practices. This way, you won't be overwhelmed by your workload while you are on the upside of your learning curve.

You should also consider the size to which you want your practice ultimately to grow. "If you don't want to be big, you don't want to grow a whole lot," Mary V. counsels. "[Then] you want three or four doctors. That's going to give you a very good income, depending on the type of doctor you have."

"We love our chiropractor," Mary adds as an example, "but I will never take on another one."

Why? "Sheer volume," Mary says. "A chiropractor can see a hundred patients a day in one fell swoop, and you've got all this paper here, whereas a neurologist sees 20 to 26 [patients per day]."

Even though both doctors bring in the same amount of money for a day's work, Mary explains, the chiropractor, billing at $30 per visit, must generate far more claims—and more work for the MIB—than the neurologist, who's billing $70 and up per visit.

What's My Niche?

OK, you've narrowed down which specialties you'll target. Now you'll want to find your niche, the unique angle that will set your business apart from—and above—the competition. This is where you can really let your creativity shine through.

Mary V. once marketed holistic health products such as vitamins and minerals along with her billing services. "What we found," she explains, "is that we are marrying that into our billing service. Both feed off the other. We were going to see this doctor's wife who called us three times since she heard about it. She wanted to get into it because he's a neurologist; he sees that this could help his patients."

Portrait of a Client

Medical billing clients come from every spectrum of every specialty. They can be retirees on their way out or handsome young hunks on their way up. Large practices contract with MIBs as often as small ones. Medical billing clients are sophisticated big-city types and small-town trenchers, HMO employees, and the self-employed.

The typical client is, however, more likely to be a doctor than a dentist, and far more likely to be a doctor than an ambulance service, pharmacy, or durable medical goods provider. He or she is likely to have been referred to the MIB by a colleague.

Other than these basics, the portrait of a typical medical billing client is delightfully blank. You can fill in just about any provider you care to go after.

Another service she offers their clients is recommendations to strengthen the business. "I had been seeing this oncologist's income just going down," the former customer service tech relates, "and I [thought] 'Well, she's billing out more. Why is her income going down?' "

Mary ran a comparison of the doctor's income between the previous and current years and determined that although the woman was billing a fair amount of money in chemotherapy drugs, she wasn't doing the amount of consultations necessary to bring in income.

"We went in with a bunch of recommendations as to what she needs to do to get that money back up," Mary explains. "We're going to set up a bunch of things to get her networking, to get her consults back up. That's how she's going to survive. She's not going to survive on drugs alone; there's just no markup there."

Starting from Retiring

The New Jersey MIB started her business closing down other people's businesses. A family friend, who also happened to be a pediatrician, asked her to take over his billing temporarily until he could find a replacement for the office manager who'd just quit. She took on the task in addition to her full-time job with the health insurance carrier.

"And then he informed me that he was going to retire in a year and he really didn't want to go through the hassle of hiring and training somebody," she says. "He asked, 'Would I like to finish up before he retired?' I said, 'Oh, what the heck.' Extra money, you know. Next thing I know, a few months later he says, 'I have this friend who lives in my development; he's a chiropractor and he really could use somebody.' "

It turned out that the chiropractor was getting ready for retirement, too, so Linda took on his billing and got him cleaned up to retire. "And I said, 'What the heck, this would be a good business to start on my own.' "

The focus of her business has changed; she now bills for mental health providers who are not retiring. But the niche she started from is an excellent example of finding a unique angle. You might want to concentrate on "cleaning up" retiring providers or on gearing up brand-new doctors who can't yet afford an in-house staff.

You might consider specializing in far-flung providers, those who live and work in remote, rural areas where there are no billing

> ### Smart Tip
>
> The Ingenix folks publish a couple of books, the *Customized Fee Analyzer* and the *National Fee Analyzer*, that show you what physicians are charging and what insurers are paying and provide data for negotiating favorable managed care contracts. They will even customize the charge rates for your zip code area. Check out www.shopingenix.com for all their products.

services. Or how about making personal service your niche? You can offer to handle your clients' noninsured patient billing as well so that you cover the full spectrum of charges and payments.

"Use your background," Mary V. suggests. "What did you do? What can you offer the office? That's really what got us thinking [about] what else we could offer."

Go the Extra Mile

You can go the extra mile, offering additional services for which, of course, you'll ask an additional fee. But at the same time, you'll be tailoring your services and making yourself and your business indispensable. Here are some ideas to kick-start your own creativity:

- *Management reports.* Give your clients up-to-the-nanosecond reports on everything that affects their productivity and income. Punch out charts and graphs on all kinds of interesting stuff: how often the doctor performs a specific procedure in a given time period; how many patients she sees on a daily, weekly, or monthly basis; how much of her business is accounted for by various insurance companies. This sort of information can be very helpful as the doctor negotiates contracts with insurers and HMOs and can be a major selling point for your service.

- *Account collections.* Put the squeeze on insurance carriers and patients for unpaid claims and bills.

- *Fee analysis.* Review your clients' fee schedules. Compare them with the reasonable and customary fees for their area and the current Medicare schedule. Suggest adjustments.

- *Secondary claims.* Send secondary claims—for example, claims in which a husband and wife are supplementally covered by each other's employer's group insurance—after the primary has paid its portion.

- *Patient statements.* Print and mail monthly statements to cash and co-payment patients. As another service, you can post them, too.

- *Patient birthdays.* Print out a monthly or quarterly list of upcoming big days so the doctor's office can send cards. Or send the cards yourself on behalf of the doctor's office.

- *Medical transcription.* Type up reports and chart notes or even medical research papers. Medical transcription is usually a service in itself and requires special training, but you can use subcontractors and offer it as a part of your package.

Up Close and Personal

Along with targeting your market—determining in which specialty you're going to start—you'll want to begin your market research.

Personal interviews are an excellent way to do this. Be sure you call first to schedule a short meeting at a time convenient to your interviewee. It's professional courtesy to presume (correctly) that other people have busy schedules. Let your subject know the reason for the interview and about how much of his or her time you expect to take, and possibly even divulge a few of the questions you'll be asking. This will put them at ease about the interview and also get them thinking ahead.

"Before I bought [my software package]," Kim H. says, "I went to our hospital administrator and to people in the area and talked to them to see if there was a need because I really wasn't familiar with the medical billing myself."

Not only did Kim discover the real need for medical billing in her area—she also made a valuable contact. "The hospital administrator [referred] me to other doctors who were moving into the area," she explains. "So I really didn't have to spend a lot of money to market myself; I was really fortunate in that aspect."

Ready, Willing, and Able

Besides going out and talking to people face-to-face, you can conduct a direct-mail survey. This serves a dual purpose: It's another way to explore your potential market, and it's a great marketing tool. While you're asking questions, you can let your future clients know that you're ready, willing, and able to take care of them.

"My initial contact with most of my contacts has been through an insurance processing claims survey," the San Diego MIB says. "I've been getting a lot of responses from chiropractors, although my target market initially was health-care providers that weren't filing electronically to Medicare."

Check with your local Medicare carrier for a list of doctors who are not filing electronically. "It came on a disc," she explains, "and all I did was just copy and paste it into my word processing program and print it up!"

Put some creativity into your surveys. You want to appear professional but at the same time informative and entertaining. Your respondents are more apt to answer a direct-mail piece that catches their attention than a poorly written one that drags. Keep your survey short and sweet. You can offer two options: a fax number for fax-return responses and a SASE (self-addressed stamped envelope) for mail-back responses.

The Economic Pulse

While you're checking out potential clients, you can start on your next task, taking your region's economic pulse.

Economically depressed areas do not generate many health-care provider visits, except perhaps for Medicaid ones, and these, as you know, are not the most highly paid. If an area shows evidence of hard times, chances are people are not spending money on doctor visits. Hence, the local medics are not going to have a lot of work for you.

If, on the other hand, the neighbors are the Range Rover-in-every-driveway type, then you can rest assured that they're health-conscious, and willing and able to spend the money necessary to stay healthy. Doctors in this neighborhood will have plenty of claims to bill.

Is your neighborhood—or one that you'd like to target—largely dependent on a nearby military base? If so, then you need to research how many of its residents get their health care free of charge at the base hospital and how many use CHAMPUS. The easiest way to do this is to call local physicians and get a ballpark estimate of how many CHAMPUS patients or families they serve.

If the neighborhood is dependent on a large industrial concern such as an auto assembly plant, then you can ascertain how many of its residents are covered by union or plant health insurance. How? Ask workers, ask neighbors, ask doctors. Call the plant's human resources department and ask them. If the plant is up and running and financially healthy, you can figure that health-care dollars will be spent. But you also need to consider—again by asking around and by reading local newspapers—whether the plant is in any danger of shutting down. A neighborhood where a large portion of the population is suddenly unemployed is not going to bode well for doctor dollars.

Bright Idea
Call your local library. Reference librarians are a veritable fount of information and amazingly helpful. Ask the librarian for local demographics. You'll be delighted at the information you receive!

You can examine your neighborhood, town, or county under the same magnifying glass, but instead of looking at the military and heavy-industry sector, check into the white-collar core. In an area like Burbank, California, for example, peopled with movie studios from Warner Bros. to Disney, a large percentage of the population has union connections and hence health-care insurance. In Rochester, New

York, everybody seems to work for Eastman Kodak. Well, you get the picture.

Have Modem, Will Cybertravel

One of the really exciting options in the MIB trade is that your business doesn't have to be restricted to your own neighborhood. Between mail, modem, and fax, you can serve just about any client anywhere.

Most medical billers serve local providers. They can build a personal relationship based on face-to-face encounters. They can run across the street or across town with material if they feel the need.

But some MIBs are experimenting with cross-country relations. The San Diego biller is working on plans to take over the billings of a company based back East. And a member of her networking group, a woman who relocated from Colorado to San Diego, still services her Colorado clients.

Stat Fact

By 2014, total health spending will make up 18.7 percent of the gross domestic product (GDP), up from the 15.3 percent Americans spent in 2003.

Direct Mail Dazzle

Use the letter on page 74 for your direct mail market survey. As you'll see, it's similar to the telephone survey of providers, only set in letter form. You can use it as is by retyping it onto your letterhead, or you can modify it in any manner that feels right to you, but keep in mind the following:

○ *Be sure to send a SASE (self-addressed stamped envelope).* This is: a) simple courtesy and b) a surer way to get your survey back than waiting on someone else's stamp.

○ *Word the letter as if you're already a going concern, not as if you're thinking about considering setting up your business.* This heightens your credibility factor—and your self-confidence as well.

○ *Make sure you've spelled the doctor's name and/or business name correctly.* Getting this one wrong is a major blooper.

○ *Make sure you have everything else spelled correctly and that your grammar and punctuation are proper.* If you're not a whiz at this kind of thing, ask someone who is to give it the once-over.

○ *Stick to the point.* Don't meander. Be punchy and snappy but not cute.

The Competition

A little competition is fine—it shows that there is a market for your services. But like Christmas cookies or New Year's Eve champagne, it's possible to have too much of a good thing. If your area is already swamped with medical billing services, you'll need to brainstorm a way to make your service different—and more appealing—than everyone else's. Of the MIBs across the country who interviewed for this book, however, this was never a problem, so don't panic. The field is still new enough, and big enough, that there seems to be plenty of room for everyone who's serious about the job.

Still, you are going to face some competition, and it's going to come from two primary sources: in-house billing clerks and other medical billing services.

The best way to compete with in-house billing is to find out as much as possible about how the typical doctor's office operates and then formulate a competitive strategy. Check out, for example, how many other responsibilities the in-house biller has. Frequently, she's also the receptionist/secretary and is signing in patients, making appointments, answering phones, and making or receiving referrals at the same time as she's handling insurance and patient billing. She's going in so many directions at once that she has little or no time to follow up on unpaid claims and no incentive to streamline, update, or expand the system.

Your marketing strategy for dealing with this type of competition is simple: You'll devote all your time to claims processing, follow-up, and billing, leaving to the office staff the important work of dealing with patients.

Nosy—Not!

Some people blanch at the thought of doing the type of research we have just discussed. It's hard enough, they feel, to approach strangers with a bunch of questions. When they factor in asking questions about the very subject they're vitally interested in, they get the small-business version of stage fright.

Don't let this happen to you. There's nothing to be nervous about. You're not being nosy; you're doing research. Plus, here's a secret: Most people love talking about themselves and their jobs. Wouldn't you? It's flattering to have someone take an interest in what you're doing.

Call a couple of medical offices and ask to speak to the person who handles the billing. You can explain exactly why you're calling. Ask if she has a couple of minutes to spare to answer your questions or, if not, find out when a good time to call back would be.

You might start with your own doctor's staff. After all, you're their client—you have a pre-existing "in."

Also keep in mind that this is a good opportunity to start marketing your services. Usually, if you're excited about your new business, other people will be, too. Don't

OLD OAK CLAIMS SERVICES

345 Main Street
Huckleberry, New Hampshire 00001
Phone (000) 000-3456
Fax (000) 000-3457

December 12, 20xx

Dr. Wally Whatsit
123 North South Street
Huckleberry, NH 00001

Dear Dr. Whatsit:

I'd like to introduce my company by asking a few questions about yours. We're in the business of helping doctors increase their patient and insurance reimbursements as well as the speed with which these payments are made.

In order to best help you, I'd appreciate your answering the following quick questions:

○ Is your office computerized? _____

○ Does your office file claims electronically? _____

○ If so, do you file only Medicare claims electronically, or do you send electronic claims to all carriers who will accept them? _____

○ How long does it usually take before you receive payment from insurance carriers? _____

○ How much does it cost you to file a claim? _____

○ How much does your office bill per month? _____

○ How much of this figure do you collect per month? _____

○ What percentage of the claims you submit are rejected? _____

○ Would your business benefit if you received payment faster and had fewer rejected claims? _____

○ Do you have an employee assigned to follow up on rejected claims?

_____

○ Would your office run more efficiently if you had someone to concentrate on billing, leaving your staff free to deal with patients? _____

be afraid to let your enthusiasm show. Hope for contagion, because at the same time you're seeking information, you'll be making valuable contacts.

You might run across some offices that have a dedicated billing clerk. This is stiffer competition, but it doesn't necessarily slam you out of the ballpark. You, after all, will be charging the doctor based on the amount of money you collect, as opposed to the in-house clerk, who gets paid a set salary whether or not she brings in reimbursements.

Shopping the Competition

As far as competition from outsource billing services, take on the challenge. Think of it as a positive rather than a negative. Here's your chance to see how others are already doing what you plan to do. Shop the competition the same way that you'd shop the mall for a new sweater. Investigate each ad in the same way you'd check out each little boutique. Peer into nooks and crannies by asking lots of questions. Compare competitors' phone personalities, management styles, specialties, and pricing structures the way you'd compare sweater weaves, styles, and prices.

You might discover when you start calling ads out of the phone book that some of your so-called competitors have gone out of business. Others might not be taking on new clients or working in the areas in which you've decided to specialize.

"Actually, all I did," the San Diego MIB says, "was look in the Yellow Pages to see if there were any listings for health-care consultants or billing services. I called them and asked a few questions about [their] pricing so I could get an average of the going rate in my area so I wasn't overpricing or underpricing myself. I asked them how long they were in business and what kind of doctors they were servicing."

She got the information she was after, but not without a few bruised feelings. She learned—as you may, too—that while most people are happy to share information, not everybody is generous.

Doctor Dialing

Stumped on what to ask in your telephone survey? At a loss for what to wonder? Fear not. On page 79, you'll find a collection of the most up-to-the-minute, topical, helpful questions to put to providers or, more correctly, their office managers or billing clerks. Make a blank copy of the worksheet for each provider you call.

When you call, remember to ask the person if this is a good time to go over a few items; if it's not, ask when a good time to call back would be.

Bright Idea

If you're an all-star at under-assertiveness and you just know you're going to screw up your approach, try this: Choose a doctor specializing in a field you don't plan to use. Call that office first. Since they're not on your list of "must-have clients," the ones you dread goofing on, your butterfly quotient will drop dramatically. You'll be amazed at how well you do! (And you might even discover you really like that office or specialty and that they're interested in you, too.)

"Some [billing services] didn't want to talk to me and then actually ended up calling their vendor," the former nurse says. "And then the vendor called me and said that that wasn't an appropriate thing to do.

"This was a vendor I had researched and ended up not going with; I don't know if that had something to do with it. But they said, 'You know, in the business world, that's not really appropriate.' Which I disagree with."

If something like this happens to you, don't take it personally. Some people are easily threatened, taking any hint of competition as a direct hit in the pocketbook or the ego.

Market Research Checklist

Don't be befuddled by market research tasks. Use this handy checklist to coordinate and organize your efforts.

Ready? Hit that target.

❑ Make a list of three markets you'd like to target (e.g., a specialty such as pediatrics or psychiatry, or a particular type of provider such as ambulance services or nursing homes).

1. _____

2. _____

3. _____

❑ Using a copy of the "Providers Survey" on page 79 for each business you plan to contact, make your calls and fill in the worksheets. Don't be shy. Call as many providers as possible.

❑ Use the direct mail piece on page 74 as a template. (You'll want to put it on your own letterhead.) Send it to as many providers as possible.

❑ Follow up phone calls and returned surveys with thank-you notes.

❑ Schedule interviews with providers, MIBs, or others in your community such as local hospital administrators.

❑ Bring a copy of your survey to use in your interviews.

❑ Follow up interviews with thank you's!

Steady? Correlate your findings.

❑ Correlate your provider information.

Do most providers in your area already outsource their billing? _____

Are most offices computerized? _____

Do most file electronic claims? _____

Of these, do most file only Medicare claims electronically? Or to all accepting carriers? _____

How long does it take for most providers to receive payment from insurers?

_____

How much does it cost most providers to file a claim? _____

What is the average monthly billable? _____

What is the average monthly collectable? _____

What percentage of claims are rejected? _____

Do most feel their businesses would benefit from your type of service? ____

How many have in-house clerks who do billing and nothing else? _____

How many seem interested in your new service? _____

Market Research Checklist, continued

❑ Correlate your billing service information.

What is an average number of clients? _____

What seem to be the most popular specialties? _____

_____

What is the average number of years in operation? _____

What is the average time to get off the ground? _____

What is the overall feeling about competition? _____

_____

What is the average pricing structure? $ _____ per claim

_____ percent

$ _____ per hour

Do most have employees? If yes, how many? _____

If so, what is the pay rate? _____

Averages of answers to your additional questions: _____

Go! Get demographics.

❑ Find out everything you can about the neighborhood, town, or county in which you wish to operate.

❑ Check with your local librarian.

❑ Get on the internet.

❑ Read local papers.

❑ Talk to your neighbors.

❑ Check with human resources or insurance departments of local large employers.

Keep going! Choose a niche.

❑ Choose three unique angles to make your business shine.

1. _____

_____

2. _____

_____

3. _____

_____

Providers Survey

Provider's business name: _____

Name and title of person giving information: _____

Phone number: _____

○ Does your office have an outsource billing service? If so, which one and why did you choose it? _____

○ If not, does your office file claims electronically? _____

○ If so, do you file only Medicare claims electronically, or do you send electronic claims to all carriers who will accept them? _____

○ How long does it usually take before you receive payment from insurers? _____

○ Is your office computerized? _____

○ Would your business benefit if you received payment faster and had fewer rejected claims? _____

○ How much does your office bill per month? _____

○ How much does your office collect per month? _____

○ What percentage of the claims you submit are rejected? Do you have an employee assigned to follow up on rejected claims? _____

○ Would your office run more efficiently if you had someone to concentrate on billing, leaving your staff free to deal with patients? _____

○ Additional questions _____

Evaluation

Now, do a personal evaluation:

○ Was the staffer you spoke with friendly? Could you ask her for advice or suggestions in the future? _____

○ Was her information in line with similar specialty providers in your area? If not, why not? _____

○ Did she provide any good tips? If so, what were they? _____

○ Were you pleased with the interview? Did you feel you handled yourself well? If not, what could you do differently with the next call? _____

✔ Did you remember to follow up with a thank-you note?

X-Ray of
a Medical
Billing Business

T his chapter could also be called "The Bare Bones"

because this is where we delve into the structure of your business

from company name to legal form to permits.

▲

Name That Business

Every business, like every child, has to have a name, and you should devote just as much thought to it. After all, you plan to have your business baby around for a long time. You want a name you can be proud of, one that identifies it—and by extension you—as worthy of your clients' confidence.

Because medical billing is a more serious-minded business than, say, pizza delivery or greeting card design, that sobriety should be reflected in your company name. This means, unfortunately for the more frivolous among us, that you can rule out names like Piglet's Claims Processing or Wild for Reimbursements.

Instead, your name should call attention to your expertise and efficiency. The terminally creative, however, can take heart. Businesslike doesn't mean dull. Your name can—and should—deliver a snappy punch.

One MIB calls her company At Your Service. "It starts with an 'A,' " she says, "which gives me a good spot in the Yellow Pages. That's my philosophy for my business. When I present myself to a physician, it's not 'These are my services and you can choose from selection A, B, or C.' It's 'What do you need to run more efficiently in your office now, and how can I be an extension to your office? How can I fill in those gaps and spaces to help your staff run more efficiently and help your whole practice be what it should be?' "

Of Surf and Scoping a Name

You have a terrific source for coming up with a business name right in your own home, probably next to the phone or buried in a drawer. It's your local Yellow Pages! Take a visual trip through the big yellow book, not just in the billing services section but in any other section that strikes your fancy. (How about advertising, architects, or boutiques?)

Do any business names conjure up an image that appeals to you? Identify that image and something similar for your business name. For example, if you see Surfside Interiors, you might consider calling yourself Surf Tide Billing Services.

If you've already come up with a name, you should check the Yellow Pages to make sure that name is not already in use. This will save you time and effort before you go for your fictitious business name. Take note, too, of any billing service names that are similar to the one you've chosen. You want your name to be truly different, to stand out from the crowd and excel, just as your business will.

Business Name Brainstorming

List three ideas based on the type of service you plan to provide (e.g., dental, quality, assured):

1. _____

2. _____

3. _____

List three ideas based on your geographic location (e.g., the name of your town, county, or state):

1. _____

2. _____

3. _____

List three ideas based on a local feature (e.g., mountain; seaside; historical reference, like Alamo; or even botanical feature, if that's what your area is known for or you like, such as Magnolia or Rose or Chaparral):

1. _____

2. _____

3. _____

Now, after you've decided which name you like the best, have you:

○ Tried it aloud to make sure it's easily understood and pronounced? (Has it passed muster with your family? Have you had a friend call to see how it sounds over the phone?)

○ Checked your local Yellow Pages to make sure the same or similar name is not already listed?

○ Checked with your local business name authority to make sure it's available?

Good! Now register it and make it your own.

Buffalo Bill(ing)

Many MIBs incorporate the name of their town or region into their business name. You might consider something like Claims Processors of Chesterfield or Billing Services of Buffalo, or you might want to incorporate a geographic or historical feature of your area, such as Seaside Services if you live at the beach or Alamo Billing and Claims if you live in San Antonio.

Whatever you go with, remember that you'll be repeating your name every time you answer the phone. Sound out the moniker before you settle on it. Some names look great in print but are difficult, if not impossible, to understand over the phone. M&A Associates, for example, may seem like a keen name for partners Marty and Andrea, but when spoken it sounds like MNA. Don't forget that most callers rate about a C-minus in listening comprehension. No matter how clearly you enunciate, they're not going to understand M&A. So save yourself hours of telephone frustration and choose something simple.

> Some names look great in print but are difficult, if not impossible, to understand over the phone.

For some really good name ideas, check out the billing services in Appendix A. You will want to make yours as individual as you are, but these will help start your creative gears turning.

The Fictitious Business Name

After you've decided on a name, you'll need to register it. Basically, registering your fictitious business name means that you check with the proper authorities to find out if someone else has already appropriated the name you want and then, assuming they haven't, pay a fee to register it as your own. If the name is already in use, you'll need to choose something different, of course.

This process varies in different regions of the country. In Florida, for example, you call the office of the secretary of state and, after a lengthy hold period, are given the opportunity to check on up to three business names. When you hit on one that hasn't been taken, the secretary's office sends you a registration form. You mail back the completed form, the registration fee, and a form from your local newspaper verifying that you've advertised your fictitious name or DBA (doing business as) for one week. In return, you receive a certificate listing your name on a nice, official-looking certificate suitable for framing.

In other areas of the country, you might simply pop down to your city or county clerk's office, thumb through the roster of business names, and then complete the registration procedure at the clerk's window.

Structuring Your Business

Use this handy checklist to make sure you've covered all the governmental regulatory bases.

Yes! I have:

❑ Filed a fictitious business name

❑ Decided on whether to become a sole proprietorship, partnership, or corporation

❑ Filed the necessary forms to become a partnership or corporation, if that's what I chose

❑ Applied for a local business license

❑ Checked into zoning regulations

❑ Complied with the following special rules, if any, that need my attention:

_____

_____

❑ Checked into local privacy laws

Your Skeletal Structure

To appease those picky IRS people, your business must have a structure. You can operate it as a sole proprietorship, a partnership, or a corporation, with variations thereon. Most medical billing services go with the simplest version, the sole proprietorship. You'll probably be starting out on your own, so there's no need to get complicated or expensive. You can always switch to another format later on if and when you take on partners and/or employees.

The Walnut Creek MIB recently restructured her business as a partnership. She had been self-employed in the field for about nine years when her accountants—who helped set up her sole proprietorship at the beginning of her MIB career—asked to become her partners.

Beware!
Just liking somebody is not a good enough reason to go into a partnership. "You've got to see what each brings to the table," Mary V. cautions. Make sure that you and your potential partner have strengths that complement each other.

▲

Mary V., who started her business as a partnership, changed gears and established a limited liability corporation (LLC) when the relationship with her business partner went sour. ("I was doing all the work," she says.) But at the beginning, the partnership worked well because the two women didn't step on each other's toes. Mary handled the customer service and technical side of the business while her partner, who had a background in insurance sales, took charge of selling. "I didn't like her side," Mary confesses, "and she hated my side." That made the blending of their skills a perfect combination.

Home Zoned Home

If you plan on a home office, you should check into zoning regulations, even though medical billing is not a business that's going to attract a lot of attention from the authorities. You won't need signage, and you'll rarely have clients knocking on your door, so you don't need to worry about parking restrictions. But it's still a good idea to play it safe. Find out from your local government whether any permits are necessary.

"I don't have people coming and going," the Montana MIB says. "I don't offer a product; I offer a service." Therefore, she met the local municipality's guidelines for residential businesses. All she was required to obtain was the usual business license.

Speaking of which, while you're querying the local authorities, you should ask about a business license. There is generally a nominal annual fee for this, but it's easier to get the license than to ignore it and worry about it in the back of your mind.

Strange Fees

The quintessential MIB rarely has to be concerned with any fees or licenses other than the ones we've just discussed. Every once in a strange while, however, something weird this way comes.

When the Walnut Creek, California, MIB started her business, "There was what we'll call a governing agency for collection agencies and billing services for the state of California," she recalls, "and their dues were $1,000 a year. To be looked upon kindly by the physicians' community, you really had to be covered by that agency, so I paid my dues. And about three months later they went out of business." Fortunately, she has a sense of humor. Also fortunately, this sort of story is extremely rare.

Loose Lips Sink Ships

While we're discussing legalese, let's go over the issue of patient confidentiality. Your doctors will trust you not only with their income but in some cases with their patients' most intimate secrets. You must uphold "your" patients' legal rights to privacy at all times, regardless of how titillating—or humdrum—you think their stories are.

Don't give in to the temptation to gab about anybody's personal, medical, or financial life to anybody except the doctor and his staff.

Become familiar with the federal and state privacy laws in your area. Your local hospital's medical records department, which must comply with stringent guidelines, or your local medical society should be able to give you information pertinent to your area.

HIPAA, HIPAA. . . Oh No!

There's an even more compelling reason these days to keep those medical records private and confidential. Just when you thought it wasn't possible for our government to dream up any more new regulations, along comes HIPAA, or the Health Insurance Portability and Accountability Act of 1996. This 500-page privacy rule was devised by the Department of Health and Human Services during the Clinton administration. It provides federal protection for personal health information so it can't be used for nonhealth purposes (like denying employment), as well as a host of other reasons. The date for full compliance with HIPAA was April 14, 2003 and April 14, 2004 for small health plans (See Appendix B).

Every vendor who comes into contact with protected health information, from MIBs to IT vendors, copy services, recyclers, shredders, and others, have to adhere to the same high standards regarding confidentiality under the provisions of HIPAA. While this may sound both ominous and labor-intensive, the reality is that MIBs are affected only slightly by the rule. The onus for protecting health information actually falls on the physician offices, hospitals, or other medical sources (known collectively as "covered entities") that provide you with the data you need for medical billing (including data provided via electronic transmission).

Under HIPAA's provisions, covered entities are required to have any vendors (like you) who handle their protected records sign a "Business Associate Contract" before sensitive health information is passed along. According to Mary Ray Brophy, Esq., a benefits attorney in the Birmingham, Michigan, law office of Clark Hill PLC, such contracts permit the covered entity to disclose protected health information to a business associate as long as the associate agrees that the information will only be used as specified in the agreement or by law. Surprisingly, however, the feds haven't yet come up with a standardized contract that would make drafting the agreement easier, although that's in the cards for the future. (The *Federal Register* has already published a proposed model contract.) So for the short term, at least, covered entities will be required to devise their own agreements, which may include the following terms and conditions:

▲

- A description of the exact way the Business Associate is permitted to use and/or disclose protected health information. For an MIB Business Associate Contract, this might be as simple as stating, "Use is restricted to coding medical conditions for the express purpose of generating a bill for each patient's insurance company."

- An agreement not to use or disclose protected health information for any reason other than the reasons listed in the Business Associate Contract. That gives the covered entity the right to terminate the contract if, say, you leak details about a famous basketball player's embarrassing health problem to a supermarket tabloid newspaper.

- A discussion of the safeguards the vendor will take when working with protected health information. For an MIB, that might mean outlining whether you have a formal security and privacy program (fairly simple for a one-person homebased business), whether you will use record encryption, how you will receive and transmit electronic data and so on.

- A guarantee that the Business Associate's own vendors (like your 17-year-old part-time file clerk or your document-shredding company) will abide by the same conditions and restrictions that the Business Associate must follow (a huge issue as it relates to your file clerk and the aforementioned basketball player).

- A host of other stuff the covered entity's legal team might deem necessary.

You can find out more information about provisions that might be included in a Business Associate Contract on the HIPAAdvisory web site at www.hipaadvisory .com/regs/privacynprm/modeba.htm. If you find yourself dateless on a Friday night, you also can try typing "Business Associate Contract" in your web browser to see what pops up. A recent attempt on the Google browser yielded more than 549,000 hits, so obviously there's plenty of information out there already. The same goes for searching on "HIPAA." Just about everyone who has anything to do with health care currently has a HIPAA link on his or her web site.

So what does all this really mean for MIBs? Not a whole lot, according to Brophy. "Obviously, medical billers will have to comply with HIPAA, but it won't be an onerous task," says Brophy, who presents seminars on HIPAA and privacy rules and their effect on employers. "While the Business Associate Contract will include a lot of requirements that billers will have to follow, if the agreements are properly drafted and enforced, most will find that all they have to do is follow good business practices." Most physician offices will have a standard contract you can sign, but it is always advisable to provide one of your own, just to cover your bases.

Some of those commonsense work practices include turning off your computer, securing access to protected documents, and otherwise safeguarding patient information on your screen when you walk away from your desk.

And just in case you're wondering, the penalties for violating HIPAA can be stiff. Fines start at $100 per violation for the inadvertent disclosure of information (like mistakenly allowing your nosy neighbor to glimpse sensitive records on your computer screen that would be of interest to the local media). On the high side, violators could face a $250,000 fine and ten years in the slammer for willful and wanton disclosure of protected information, such as selling protected information to a person who's fact-finding for a client involved in a malpractice suit.

> "Obviously, medical billers will have to comply with HIPAA, but it won't be an onerous task."

The bottom line is, "Don't slip up—do the HIPAA!"

Your Business Gurus

It never hurts to consult an attorney and accountant for tips on how to proceed with your business structure. Your attorney and accountant will be able to help you determine what is best for your particular situation.

You'll also want an attorney to look over the contracts you'll be signing with doctors and to advise you on any special concerns (read "worries and anxieties")—like malpractice, a doctor or government entity accusing you of fraudulent coding or billing, or a patient who sues for no good reason.

Don't forget your insurance agent. She can ease the same worries and concerns by providing errors and omissions coverage as well as special protection for your business equipment.

We've given you an X-ray of the typical medical billing service's skeleton. The licenses, fees, and structures discussed are the only ones you should need to worry about.

6

Pain Management
Figuring Your Finances

That old refrain "The best things in life are free" does not quite apply when you're starting a business. This chapter, therefore, dips into the murky waters of budgeting, financing, and operating costs and, like chlorine, clears them up.

Start-Up Costs

One of the many nifty things about a medical billing service is that its start-up costs are comparatively low. You have the advantage of establishing a homebased business, which cuts office lease expenses down to nothing. You have almost no inventory, which means no outlay of funds for pretty doodads to grace display spaces (and in fact, you have no display spaces!). Your major financial outlay will be for office equipment and your software and/or business opportunity since, if you're like many moderns, you already have a computer.

But let's take it from the top. The following is a breakdown of everything—from heavy investment pieces to flyweight items—you'll need to get up and running:

- Computer system with modem and printer
- Fax machine
- Software and/or business opportunity
- Clearinghouse
- Reference materials
- CMS 1500 forms
- Phone
- Voice mail or answering machine
- Stationery and office supplies
- Postage

You can add all kinds of goodies of varying degrees of necessity onto this list, and we'll cover all of them in depth in Chapter 9—a sort of shopping bonanza. For example, a copier is a plus. It's also nice to have bona fide office furniture: a tweedy upholstered chair with lumbar support that swivels and rolls, gleaming file cabinets that really lock, real oak bookshelves.

But let's consider that you're starting absolutely from scratch. You can always set up your computer on your kitchen table or on a card table in a corner of the bedroom. You can stash files in cardboard boxes. It's not glamorous, but it'll suffice until you get your business steaming ahead. You can garner patient materials by post instead of by fax, as some MIBs have opted to do.

Computing Computer Costs

It's highly recommended that you have a computer system—you can't do anything with fancy billing software if you don't have the hardware to run it. Although we don't recommend it, it is possible to start off without electronics—which will save you some dough—but if you opt for this method, you're asking to do things the hard way.

The New Jersey MIB began her business on the typewriter in her retiring pediatrician's office. "It was horrible," she says, laughing. "But you know what? I really didn't mind it. We used ledger cards and a pegboard, the whole works, but I really didn't mind it. It worked."

For a basic computer system—monitor, mouse, modem, hard drive, and printer—you should allocate around $1,500 to $2,000. We'll go over all the permutations in the next chapter, but this will give you a figure to pencil in for starters.

Fax Facts

Although technically you don't have to have a fax machine, just as you don't have to have a computer, your MIB life will run much more smoothly with one. You can shoot off and receive materials to and from doctors, carriers, and patients instead of waiting on the postal service. Sending a claim follow-up by fax, for example, has a lot more impact on the insurer when it directly follows your call. You can purchase a basic plain-paper fax machine for as little as $100.

The Skinny on Software

Software prices can vary radically, depending on which medical claims billing package you buy and from whom. This is an area to which you should devote a great deal of research. You're going to be virtually married to your program, spending hours of quality time with it, and you want to be sure you and your software are a match made in microprocessing heaven. Again, this is a subject we'll discuss in depth in Chapter 9.

Let's say here that you'll want to allocate somewhere between $500 and $5,000, depending on many variables, including whether you purchase just the MIB software or the business opportunity to go with it.

The MIB in New Jersey started with low-end software. While she was still in typewriter mode, she happened upon a catalog and began flipping through it. "I went to the Medical Arts Press catalog and I picked software for $499—didn't even know the name of it—and had it shipped," she laughs. "I don't know if I was brave or ignorant. I didn't actually know there were other people doing medical insurance billing."

After she'd been up and running a while with the "blind date" software and became more industry-savvy, she switched to a full business opportunity/software package.

Clearinghouse Costs

Clearinghouses, like software, require research on your part. If the software is like a marriage partner or significant other, then the clearinghouse is the brother or sister-in-law that comes to visit for what seems to be the rest of your life. You'd better be sure you're happy living under the same roof with it.

Also like software, clearinghouse costs vary radically. You should allocate from zero to $300 for "membership" fees and from zero to $50 per doctor for sign-up.

By Way of Reference

Although your reference library can comfortably contain a wealth of texts, we'll consider here only the very few that are real must-haves, the ICD-10, CPT, and HCPCS 2007 Level II Expert coding books. If you're billing for dentists, you'll also want the CDT-3, which is the dental version of CPT codes. You can sketch in about $83 for a single download of CPT or around $229 if you have a small staff of under 10 people and wish to network the software. The physical book costs around $99. Figure on spending around $95 for the HCPCS 2007 Level II Expert and considerably more for the ICD-10 Second Edition ($1035 for the book with CD, $342 for the downloadable version). The CDT book will set you back about $52 and some change.

Phone Fun

We assume that you already have a telephone, in which case you already know all about phone bills. You should, however, install at least one separate dedicated line for your business, preferably two. You'll want one line for handling phone calls and another for your electronic billing, unless you plan to transmit all your information late at night or in the wee hours of morning. Computers use phones the way teenagers do—when they're transmitting, no one else can possibly get through. So unless you want to risk having callers receive a busy signal or empty ring when you're e-mailing claims, you'll want to have a separate line.

Costs, of course, depend on how many fun features you add to your telephone service and which local and long-distance carriers you go with, but for the purpose of start-up budgeting, let's say you should allocate about $25 per line. You'll also need to add the phone company's installation fee, which should be around $40. Check with your local Ma Bell (or one of her deregulated relatives) to determine exactly what these costs are in your area.

Please Leave a Message

You will occasionally want to escape from your telephone—when you're out seeing clients, running errands, or (when you have everything caught up) skipping off to the movies. During these times, you will need somebody or something to answer your phone. A Murphy's Law of Business Life is that people call most often when: a) you are not in your office, b) you are sitting down to a meal, or c) you are in the shower. Another business life law is that an unanswered phone is extremely unprofessional.

You have two ways to go here: the trusty answering machine or the phone company's voice-mail feature. Both have pros and cons, which we'll discuss in Chapter 9. For estimating start-up costs, let's figure a basic answering machine at about $40 and voice mail at about $6 a month.

Office Supplies

Business stationery is as important to a crisp, efficient image as a professionally-answered phone. To create that efficient identity—which will be one of your biggest selling points—you'll need letterhead, envelopes, and business cards. There are a lot of routes to take with all this stuff.

Let's say, however, that to create the basics, you can purchase blank stationery, including cards, and print them up yourself with your word processing or desktop publishing program. Or you can have a set of business cards inexpensively printed for you at a quick-print house like Kinko's or at Office Depot's in-house service.

"I spent $49 for a thousand business cards," the Virginia MIB says. "I maybe have used, I would say, not over 20 of them. The rest of it's been word-of-mouth."

Office supplies—pens, pencils, paper clips, colored pickup folders or mailing envelopes for your clients, reams of blank paper for designing brochures or fliers, stapler, staples, letter opener, tape, printer cartridges—can be penciled in at about $150. This is, of course, if you start from absolute scratch, buying everything brand new for your business. CMS 1500 forms go for less than $35 for a box of 2,500.

> ### Smart Tip
> If your budget can stretch that far, it's a good idea to talk to an accountant and an attorney. They can advise you on tax issues before tax time, make sure your client contract is up to snuff and generally keep you out of trouble.

> ### Dollar Stretcher
> Scrounge around your home. You probably have lots of these office supplies accumulating in drawers just waiting to be put to use.

Postage

We're not talking the Victoria's Secret catalog mailroom here. Your postage costs will be fairly low, but you do need to tally them into your start-up costs. How much you spend depends a great deal on what you expect to be doing. If you supply each doctor with a $4.60 priority mail envelope each week, as the San Diego MIB does, then your costs to receive material will run about $19.78 a month (at 4.3 weeks in a month) per doctor. If you figure paper claims and patient statements at 300 pieces per doctor per month, then you'll be spending another $123 per month (one 41-cent stamp per piece) to mail out statements.

You can also figure on 41 cents per brochure. If you send out five a week, you will spend roughly another $8.82 a month.

Postage Meters and Internet Postage

Once your business is up and running, you're liable to be handling a lot of outgoing mail, including bills sent to clients and brochures sent to new prospects. So a postage meter can be a huge time-saver. Not only does it eliminate those annoying and nonproductive trips to and from the post office (not to mention the long waits in line), but it also saves you from licking and sticking stamps on envelopes.

You have a couple of options when it comes to buying postage. You can lease a standard postage meter, which requires you to pay a monthly mailing fee of $15 to $50, then pay for postage upfront at the post office. Or you can forgo leasing altogether by buying your postage online from providers like Pitney Bowes (see Appendix A). For a modest fee (usually no more than $4.95 per month) above the actual cost of the postage, you can download software that allows you to print your postage directly onto labels. You can charge the cost of the postage to any credit card.

You also may need a postal scale to make sure you're affixing enough postage to your outgoing mail. A 41-cent stamp covers letters of up to 1 ounce, which is roughly three to four pages of letter-sized paper. Anything over that requires additional postage. Some of the online companies will provide you with a postal scale free or for a nominal charge. Otherwise, you can expect to pay $10 to $25 for a mechanical scale (which is useful if you mail up to 12 items a day) or $50 to $200 for a digital scale for sending 12 to 24 items per day. If you send more than 24 items a day or use priority or expedited mailing services on a regular basis, you should consider purchasing a programmable electronic scale, which runs $80 to $250.

Adding It All Up

Use the worksheet on page 103 to pencil in and then tally up all your costs. If you copy a couple of extra sheets first, you can compare various options, decide which will work the best for you, and then arrive at your "Official Start-Up Figure."

The New Jersey MIB estimates her original start-up costs at close to $5,000 or $6,000. She is not including her final choice software package in this figure because she purchased it after she'd already been up and running.

The Montana MIB puts her start-up costs in the same range. With this amount, she was able to purchase her training, software, computer, and the necessary office furniture.

The former pastor's costs were higher. Figuring in purchasing a fax machine, upgrading his existing home office, and spending about $700 to print brochures, he weighs in his total start-up at just a little more than $10,000.

Talking Money

Now that we've determined how much it's going to cost you to get your business up and running, let's turn to the fun part—figuring out how much money you can expect to make.

Medical billing services charge their clients by three methods: percentage, per claim, and hourly. The percentage basis is generally used by MIBs who do full-practice management or a combination of patient billing and claims billing and, just as it sounds, the MIB charges the provider a percentage of the money he *collects* per month as opposed to the amount of money he *bills*.

"We charge [the doctors] on collected revenues, not on their production levels," the Walnut Creek, California, MIB explains. "The money all comes to us and we put it into their own personal checking accounts and then I will bill them, depending on how big the practice is, sometimes twice a month, sometimes once a month. And they pay the bill in a timely manner or we stop doing their work."

The percentages you'll charge will depend on several variables: the going rate in your part of the country, the sorts of procedures your doctors are providing, and their patient volume.

"I take a lot of things into consideration," Maryland-based Mary V. says. "With what I know about certain things, I'll charge the doctor a different percentage on the type of claim that it is. I charge a different percentage for workers' comp, for personal injury. If they handle a lot of cash, I'll actually drop that percentage because I know I'm not going to have to bill that out. All I'm going to do is data entry. One doctor might have four different percentages. With experience, I know now how much time certain claims take. With personal injury, it might be six years before that case is settled."

Since personal injury cases take so long to pay, Mary charges a higher percentage of the claim, usually 10 percent and above, whereas routine Medicare claims are billed at anywhere from 5 percent to 10 percent.

With all these variables, estimating an annual income might seem like a task fit for a professor of Boolean mathematics, but it's not really difficult. In fact, it's fun! (Adding up numbers is always more interesting when it pertains to money in your bank account.)

Here's what you do: First, settle on an average percentage. Let's use 7 percent, which is the fee the San Diego MIB charges.

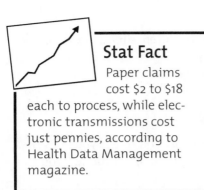

Stat Fact

Paper claims cost $2 to $18 each to process, while electronic transmissions cost just pennies, according to Health Data Management magazine.

Next, estimate how much one client will collect in a year. This is tough, starting cold, because you don't have any clients to base your figures on. If you've done your homework, however, you'll have an idea of how much money doctors in your target market are billing and collecting per month.

Let's say your first doctor collects a nice round figure of $15,000 per month, which multiplied by 12 months gives him an annual collectable income of $180,000. His billable income might be far more, and this, of course, is where you come in—your mission being to bring his billable and collectable into alignment.

Now, all you have to do is multiply this $180,000 current collectable figure by 7 percent, which gives you a potential annual income of $12,600. We say "potential" because this sum, as we've just explained, can improve dramatically once you're at the helm. For example, if you're able to increase the doctor's collectable income by 10 percent, he'll now be bringing in $198,000 per year, which will give you $13,860 per year.

If you increase your client base by another five providers, each with the same collectable income, you're suddenly grossing $83,160 per year.

Per-Claim Jumping

Some MIBs prefer to charge on a per-claim basis rather than by percentage. This is the method of choice for billers whose workload consists mainly of straight claims billing with little or no practice management tasks.

"I bill per claim," says the Illinois MIB. "The offices do the front-end data entry and I do the back-end tweaking and electronic filing and some of the follow-up work. I'm charging right now anywhere from $1 to $3 per claim."

In rural Virginia, the teacher charges $2.50 per insurance claim and $1.75 per patient invoice, which she feels is probably average in her area. Up in suburban New Jersey, another MIB charges $3 to $5 per claim.

When you charge via this method, you charge per claim billed rather than per claim collected. You will want to charge the going rate in your area, which you'll have determined through the market research we discussed in Chapter 4. Since you'll also have determined through your research how many

▲

Reserves, Not Just for Feds

Some medical billing services take off immediately, usually because they have built-in business; i.e., someone who's already requested their services. Others struggle for months before landing that first client. If you have providers already lined up, you can skip this section. But if you're starting cold with the only active clients the ones in your mind's eye, then you'll need to determine what sort of financial reserves will be necessary to keep you eating until your business gets going.

It took the San Diego MIB five months to land her first client. This is not unusual in this business. In fact, it's a given that nabbing those first doctors is a tough proposition. Unless you have a trust fund or a significant other bringing home the bacon, don't quit your day job.

With a brand-new client in the stable, the former nurse is figuring an average monthly gross of about $700 and operating expenses of under $150. Kim H., who's still working as a teacher, earns $800 to $1,000 a month with minimal monthly expenses and is not yet prepared to give up her day job.

claims doctors in your area are filing each month, you'll have a good basis for determining your annual gross income.

Let's say your first doctor is billing 350 claims per month, which, multiplied by 12 months, comes to 4,200 claims. If you charge $3 per claim, your gross annual income will be $12,600. Now, if you take on another five physicians, your gross jumps to $75,600.

Counting the Hours

The third, and least popular, method of charging clients is per hour. "I think it would be a really hard selling feature for doctors," says the San Diego biller. "They're already paying somebody on an hourly basis. Why would they want to hire somebody outside the office and pay them hourly as well?"

You might want to consider this option if you have a client whose billing rate is so low that charging per claim or on a percentage basis is not feasible. Or you might run into a client who is comfortable working under this arrangement and does not want to deviate from her norm.

Again, your market research will be the key to determining an hourly charge. Here is one way to determine an hourly rate. Let's take an average of your annual fee for one doctor, based on the per-claim and percentage methods we used above. This will give us an annual gross income of $13,000. Now, if we divide this by 12 months, we get $1,083 per month. Assuming that your client supplies only 40 hours of work a month, you end up with an hourly charge of $27.

(Note that these are all hypothetical figures. You may far exceed these numbers, or you may find that your economic region, your level of expertise, or the amount of work you choose to do puts your income somewhere below what we've given.)

Operating Expenses

OK, we've had a ball counting chickens. Now it's time to swing the pendulum the other way and calculate your operating expenses. These, subtracted from your projected gross income, will tell the true tale of how much you'll be making.

We will assume once again that you are going to be homebased, so we won't worry about expenses for office rent or utilities. However, we do need to think about the following:

- Phone
- Postage
- Stationery and office supplies
- Clearinghouse
- Loan repayment
- Online service

The MIBs interviewed for this book feel that their operating expenses are minimal. "I would say that I can run everything for less than $200 a month," the MIB in Montana says, "and that would include postage, paper, telephone. I have very few expenses."

The Illinois MIB says, "Now that I've got pretty much everything I needed, [my operating expenses] are low. It really just depends on how many claims I process because obviously the clearinghouses charge you per claim. So if you take that out of the picture, it's pretty much just a bigger phone bill." He estimates his monthly phone charges, with three lines, at about $80 a month.

The first three items on the list—phone, postage, and stationery/supplies—have been

---

Mix 'n' Match

The great fun of all these charge methods is that you can mix and match methods and rates, customizing each doctor's contract. "Most everything I do is per claim," the New Jersey MIB says. "But I do have two psychiatrists on a percentage basis, between 7 [percent] and 9 percent. I base every practice differently."

You can beef up your monthly charges—and cover some of your start-up expenses—by customizing other featured services for your providers. You can charge your doctors a one-time setup fee for entering their patients into your software program. You could accomplish this by charging a flat fee, say $300, the same setup fee you may be charged by your clearinghouse. This will neatly cancel out one start-up expense from your list. Or you might charge your doctors per existing patient, say $4 each. If each doctor in your stable of six has an average of 400 patients, then you've added $9,600 of extra income.

---

covered in this chapter's start-up section. Your monthly operating expenses should be about the same as we've discussed.

Cuckoo for Clearinghouses

Your clearinghouse expenses will be different. Once you pay your origination fee and your per-doctor fee, you'll be looking at the per-claim fee. If, for example, the clearinghouse you choose charges 50 cents per claim and you plan to route through 150 claims per month, then you'll need to pencil in $75.

All of this is subject, of course, to any number of variations. For instance, the Montana MIB's clearinghouse charges a flat fee of $40 for an unlimited number of claims. The Maryland MIB's clearinghouse charges 35 cents per claim. And the clearinghouse used in conjunction with one business opportunity vendor has no fees unless you process fewer than 400 claims per month.

Keep in mind that not all your claims will be sent electronically, and of those that are, not all will go through a clearinghouse. You can bill directly to Medicare and the Blues.

Paying the Piper

We've set aside an operating expense called loan repayment. If you don't borrow money to start your business, you won't need this one. If, however, you finance your start-up costs through any means, you'll need to repay the piper, and here's where you pencil in whatever your monthly fee is.

Start-Up Expenses

Check out the start-up costs (in other words, the costs to officially throw open the door) for two hypothetical billing services: Check-Up Medical Billing and Health-Care Help Services. Check-Up is a homebased company (office in the spare bedroom) whose owner is retired and decided to start out small with a minimum outlay. Health-Care, on the other hand, has rented a 500-square-foot downtown office, purchased top-of-the-line equipment, and employed a part-time assistant. Check-Up is projecting annual gross collections of $16,800; Health-Care's annual projection is $42,000. Neither owner draws a salary; instead, they take a percentage of their net profits as income.

Expenses	Check-Up Medical Billing	Health-Care Help Services
Rent (security deposit and first month)	$N/A	$1,000.00
Office equipment, furniture, & supplies	3,083.00	8,905.00
Postage meter (rent for one year)	N/A	180.00
MIB software	700.00	N/A
MIB software/business opportunity package	N/A	5,000.00
Clearinghouse start-up fees	300.00	N/A
CMS 1500 forms	35.00	35.00
Licenses	150.00	150.00
Phone	90.00	115.00
Utility deposits	N/A	150.00
Employee wages	N/A	875.00
Grand opening advertising	100.00	500.00
Legal services	375.00	525.00
Insurance	500.00	600.00
	$5,368.00	$17,990.00
Miscellaneous expenses (add roughly 10% of total)	$537.00	$1,799.00
Total Start-Up Costs	**$5,870.00**	**$19,834.00**

Start-Up Expenses Worksheet

Rent (security deposit and first month)   \$_____

Office equipment and furniture
  (see MIB Office Checklist on page 137)   _____

MIB software/business opportunity   _____

Clearinghouse start-up fees   _____

Reference materials   _____

CMS 1500 forms   _____

Phone service   _____

Utility deposits   _____

Employees   _____

Grand opening advertising   _____

Legal and accounting services   _____

Insurance   _____

Miscellaneous expenses   _____

Official Start-Up Figure   \$_____

Olé for Online Service

This expense is a must-have if you want to take advantage of the ease and afford-ability of online claim processing. Again, your costs will depend on which service you go with and what rate you choose, but the majority have given up on competing rate-wise and routinely charge \$20-\$25 a month for unlimited usage.

Putting It All Together

You can use the worksheet on page 107 to pencil in your projected income and estimated operating expenses. You may have many more expenses than the ones discussed here, such as yearly coding upgrades, seminars and their requisite travel

> **Tip...**
>
> ## Smart Tip
>
> No one can tell you how many claims any client will generate—there are too many variables. But Tammy Harlan, president of Santiago SDS Inc., a medical billing business opportunity, says the average family practice doctor has approximately 500 claims per month.

expenses, employees and their requisite workers' compensation insurance, pension plans, auto expenses, subscription fees for professional journals, butler and maid service (just dreaming!), and pizza delivery or Chinese take-out costs. We've put in rent, utilities, employee, and insurance costs, but obviously, if these don't apply to you, don't worry about them.

Once you've calculated your estimated operating expenses you can subtract them from your calculated earnings and–voilà!–you have a projected income/expense total.

Help from Your Friends

Now that you've done all the arithmetic, you can determine just how much you'll need to get started. Why, then, you may ask, did I have to go through all the work of figuring out my net income?

Good question. The answer is that, first off, you'll now have determined that it's worth borrowing money to get started in this business. And secondly, you can show all these beautifully executed figures to your borrower to show him or her that your business is a good risk and that you'll be able to repay the loan without difficulty.

Another of the many joys of the medical billing service is that its start-up costs are relatively low. Some MIBs were able to finance themselves with assistance only from a friendly little plastic rectangle.

"I had a partner when I first got into the business and we financed it using credit cards," Mary V. says. "Nobody would give us a loan, so it was credit cards. My partner and I were sitting one night [working] and somebody called us from my alma mater and said, 'We want you to have a credit card,' and I thought 'Wow, OK!' That's how we started. That's how we bought a lot of things."

The Montana MIB went the same route. "I went ahead and put [the start-up financing] on a card with a very low interest rate, and it was less than I could have received a business loan for," she says.

"I was in a slightly different situation from most people," the Walnut Creek MIB recalls of her start-up financing experiences 14 years ago. "I had just completed a divorce, we had done our financial settlement and we had sold a house, so I took the money from the house and put it in the business." But it still wasn't enough.

"I couldn't find funding," the former nurse says. "I was a female with no business experience. So I just went on a wing and a prayer."

When her accountants—the ones who have since become her partners—first heard her plans, their reaction was "Oh my God, you'll never make it. It's not possible, you're underfunded."

"And I really was underfunded," the Walnut Creek MIB adds. "It was a huge struggle, but I had two employees who knew me, who knew how well I could do, and put their total faith in me, left good secure jobs to come with me. And I didn't take a salary for almost a year. It was kind of interesting. It was a true struggle, but I managed to land a very, very good client, an orthopedic group with five doctors on board who understood what I was trying to do and who hung in there with me."

The Illinois MIB financed his start-up by going to a familiar source: his father. He didn't have to do a big sales pitch, he says. "I let him know what I was doing and why I wanted to do it."

Most MIBs, like the ex-pastor, are self-financed, via VISA or MasterCard, relatives, or on-hand cash.

Dollar Stretcher

Now might be the time to take advantage of those credit card solicitations that seem to arrive in the mail daily. Most feature very low introductory rates, which can be used as a springboard for your start-up (but not for a new wardrobe or the latest DVD player)!

Romancing the Bank

You might want to consider financing through your bank or credit union. In this case, your start-up cost and income figures are extremely important. The bank will want to see all of this, neatly laid out and carefully calculated. You'll also want to show them your mission statement and any figures you can present—for instance, the ones in this book—about the bright future of the medical billing industry.

If you do go with a bank, it may pay to think small. "Small banks traditionally are better for small businesses because they're always looking for ways to accommodate these customers," said Wendy Thomas, senior business consultant at the Michigan Small Business Development Center in Detroit. "Small banks may be more willing to deal with small-business concerns and are more sensitive to issues like the need for longer accounts receivable periods."

Instead of shooting for a straight business loan, the prospective MIB could go for a home equity loan or borrow against a vehicle that's paid for or a savings or CD account. Don't discount your home as a cash cow—you might be surprised to learn how much equity you actually have.

Get the lowdown on getting financing for your business—from friends and family to credit cards and bank loans.

Operating Income/Expenses

Take a look at this sample Operating Income/Expenses. We've provided a work-sheet on page 107. Use it to compute your projected income and expenses.

Projected Monthly Income $3,000.00

Projected Monthly Expenses

Phone service	$25.00
Postage	50.00
Miscellaneous expenses *(stationery and office supplies)*	50.00
Rent	400.00
Utilities	50.00
Employees	240.00
Advertising	100.00
Clearinghouse fees	120.00
Insurance	90.00
Loan repayment	100.00
Online service	20.00
Total Expenses	−$1,245.00
Projected Income/Expense Total	**$1,755.00**

Note: *Sound accounting practice dictates that you allow six months operating expenses as your suggested operating capital.*

Operating Income/Expenses Worksheet

Projected Monthly Income $_____

Projected Monthly Expenses

    Phone service $_____

    Postage   _____

    Miscellaneous expenses
      (stationery and office supplies)   _____

    Rent   _____

    Utilities   _____

    Employees   _____

    Advertising   _____

    Clearinghouse fees   _____

    Insurance   _____

    Loan repayment   _____

    Online service   _____

      Total Expenses $ –_____

    Projected Income/Expense Total $_____

Note: *Sound accounting practice dictates that you allow six months operating expenses as your suggested operating capital*

Medical Center or House Calls

Locating Your Business

As we've said many times, one of the great perks of running a medical billing service is that it lends itself ideally to the homebased entrepreneur. It doesn't require a high-traffic or high-visibility location and doesn't need to be in the trendy part of town or in an industrial complex, although those are certainly options. You don't need a mahogany-paneled office

▲

with a lobby and conference room to impress or entertain clients. The only space requirement is an area large enough for your desk, your chair, a few filing cabinets, and perhaps a bookshelf.

It's convenient—you couldn't get any closer to your office unless you slept with your computer. It's economical—you don't need to spend money on leased space, extra utilities, transportation costs, or lunches down at the corner grill.

Working at home is not, however, mandatory. You may want to leave your laundry, your dog, and/or your kids/spouse at home while you go off to an office space that's nice, quiet, clean, and yours alone.

The Home Office

If you choose to be homebased, you can locate your office work space anywhere in the house that's convenient. Most homebased MIBs have a dedicated office that's reserved just for the business. You could locate your home office in a den, a FROG (finished room over garage), the garage itself, the recreational vehicle parked in the backyard (so long as you run electrical and phone lines out to it), or a corner of the kitchen. Keep in mind that whatever space you choose will be your workstation and command center. If you have a boisterous family, a cubbyhole in your bedroom might be much more conducive to quiet, clear thinking than a nook in the den with the big-screen TV blaring at all hours. Also remember that yelling into the phone over cartoon kerblams and pows will not make you sound particularly professional to your clients.

The Tax Man Speaketh

Another advantage to the home office is, as the former bookkeeper says, the ability to write it off as a home business. The IRS will graciously allow you to deduct money from your income taxes if you're using a portion of your home as your income-producing work space. You can deduct a percentage of expenses equivalent to the percentage of space your home office occupies. If, for example, you're using one room in an eight-room house, you can deduct one-eighth of your rent or mortgage payment plus one-eighth of your utility bills off your taxes. You can also deduct based on the square footage used for business out of the total of your house or apartment.

There is, of course, an *if* involved here. You can use this deduction if you're using this space solely as your office. If you've turned your spare bedroom into your office and you don't use it for anything but conducting your business, then you qualify. If, however, your office is tucked into a corner of the kitchen and you're still feeding people in there, you do not qualify for the home office deduction (unless you can convince the IRS that you order Chinese every night and the refrigerator is actually a file cabinet).

Growing Pains

As your business grows, you may find that your dedicated office has become a dedicated house—and that it's time to move up to commercial office space. Because the medical billing service doesn't rely on client traffic or a prestigious address, any area that appeals to you and your pocketbook is up for grabs. It's a good idea to look into an inexpensive office space, off the pricier main drag. Even better is the second or third floor of a commercial building such as a bank or insurance company. These buildings always have space available and are less expensive than space in a high-traffic retail area, which is perfect because you don't need high visibility anyway.

Let's Make a Deal

Locating that gem of an office requires as much as ingenuity and forethought as researching your market. But a little chutzpah pays off.

When the Walnut Creek MIB started her business, she wanted to locate in a commercial space. "I knew the landlord of this building and that it was underoccupied," she says. "It was a great, quiet location that I thoroughly enjoyed. We had a park out of one set of windows and a church out of the other one. It was just very peaceful there.

"So I went and talked to him and told him what I was trying to do and negotiated an excellent rent. He always said that he lost money on me being there. I signed a lease for three years with great hope and all fingers crossed. He was fabulous. Even after that lease ran out, he still gave me an excellent rent. I had started out with just one suite, but when we expanded I ended up with three. So I was a pretty good bet for him."

Don't be afraid to negotiate. Like the Walnut Creek MIB, you just might end up with the deal of a lifetime. Be honest. Let the prospective landlord know what you can afford. Offer your best bet. If he doesn't go for it, ask what concessions he can make. If you can't come to an agreement, thank him for his time and bid him a fond farewell. There are plenty of other office spaces in the sea.

Alternative Officing

If commercial office space is not your bag, you might consider a more unconventional approach. Rent a house or an apartment (providing you check the zoning laws first). This may present an advantage over an office suite because of the private kitchen and bathroom. If you already live

Bright Idea

Tap your local commercial real estate broker for info and advice. Besides giving you the rental lowdown in your town, he can act as a terrific referral for potential clients for you. A good realtor knows everybody in town and usually has a stable of doctors as his own clients.

in an apartment, you may choose to rent another unit in the same building to use as your office. You can walk to work. And the landlord may give you a package deal—or a finder's fee!

Take a space over a storefront downtown. How about over a coffeehouse or doughnut shop or bagel bakery? What better incentive to get to work in the morning!

Or strike up a deal with a doctor. You bill a certain amount of work for him in exchange for office space. This arrangement might especially appeal to a physician who's just starting out in business himself.

The Medical Complex

The medical complex is the high-rent district. But don't bypass the high-density doctor zone without a thought. Get creative. Try negotiating with the leasing agent, especially if you can find a new complex. Point out that your business can be a draw for doctors considering the suites.

The major draw for you to locate in a medical complex is, of course, convenience, both for your clients and for yourself. This is especially true if you are going to be doing full-practice management. When patients visit the doctor, you will be readily available to answer questions, get insurance precertification, or field complaints.

Doctors and their staff will have easy access to you and your office. They won't have to fax or mail superbills or patient information, plus they can sneak over for a cup of java and a sympathetic ear when the patient crush gets too traumatic.

On the plus side for you, you don't have to drive to pick up billing materials and, as new doctors come on the scene, you'll already be there as the answer to their billing prayers. On the negative side, you'll have commuter woes, the added expense of a lease and all those meal decisions—sack lunch, corner café, or takeout.

Bright Idea
Don't come out of the closet—go into it! Some homes, especially older ones, have walk-in closets—some with windows—that are large enough to turn into a cozy little office. Just make sure yours has adequate ventilation and light.

Portrait of a Home Office

If you opt for the home office, it's important to remember that you are still a professional. Your work quarters—like you—should be organized and efficient. If at all possible, designate a separate room with four walls and a door. Aim for pleasant, quiet, well-lit surroundings. You're going to be spending a lot of time in this space, so you want it to be comfortable.

First Impressions

Even if your office is in your garage, your business still needs a professional image. But instead of worrying about the right shade of charcoal for your clients' chairs, arranging the seating for that just-right aura of subliminal authority, or choosing signed lithographs for the walls, you can create your professional image through your business cards, stationery, and logo.

You can do it all yourself with desktop publishing. But, as with deciding on a business name, be sure that the image you're beaming into the minds of prospects and clients is the one you want. Leave the over-the-top-trendy or oh-so-cutesy images for other businesses. A logo featuring dancing skeletons with mariachis won't quite cut it, and unless you're specializing in pediatrics and pediatrics alone, a cuddly teddy bear is not the best logo, either.

Your most important goal with your printed materials is to convey the impression of brisk, organized efficiency and expertise. This is what you're selling. Have a friend or family member look over your designs before you commit to a print run of 500 cards or letterhead. Do they see typos? Amateurishness? Or do they catch the gleam of a business riding the waves of proficiency?

If you can't carve out a dedicated space, by all means take over a corner of another room. But consider it your permanent office. Clearing your work materials off the dining room table before every meal is a definite drag.

Appropriate a desk or table large enough to hold your computer, keyboard, phone, and pencil holder, stapler, etc., and still have enough room to spread out your working papers. A charming 19th century cherry-wood secretary looks great but probably will not allow enough space for several stacks of files plus you and your computer. Don't skimp on elbow room.

Commandeer a comfortable chair, one that fits under the desk with enough legroom for you to stretch out. Make it as cushy as possible. Your posterior and the seat of that chair are going to be in close contact for many, many hours, and a sturdy kitchen chair is going to feel like concrete in short order.

You should have a file cabinet or two, or at least a set of cardboard file boxes. Place them close at hand but not underfoot. It's no fun digging through the back of the clothes closet or running out to the garage every time somebody calls with a question. You should also have a bookcase or shelf to hold your reference library. Again, make it as convenient as possible.

Make Yourself at Home

Use this handy worksheet to locate and design your home office.

List three possible locations in your home:

1._____

2. _____

3. _____

Make a physical survey of each location.

❏ Are phone and electrical outlets placed so that your equipment can easily access them? Or will you be faced with unsightly, unsafe cords snaking across the carpet?

❏ Will your current desk or table or the one you have your eye on fit? Measure your space carefully to be sure.

❏ Do you have adequate lighting? If not, can you create or import it?

❏ Is there proper ventilation?

❏ What is the noise factor?

❏ Is there room to spread out your work?

Optional:

❏ How close is it to the coffee maker? Refrigerator? (This can be either a plus or minus, depending on your current waistline and jitter factor.)

The Outside Office

If you plan to locate your office in a medical complex, you'll want to think about visitors. In this case, your bricks-and-2 x 4s bookcase and the milk-crate filing cabinet from college are not your best option. You'll want "real" office furniture that conveys the impression of clean, quiet efficiency. It doesn't need to be fancy, but it should be pleasant and comfortable.

Bright Idea

If your closet is of the sliding-doors/runs-along-one-wall variety, take out the clothes and stash them somewhere else. Remove the doors, and you have a dandy office nook.

Your visitors will, for the most part, be on the run, but you can provide a chair or two on which to alight. You'll also want that American office altarpiece, the coffee maker, and if you can provide a tidbit or two—homebaked cookies or a jar of candies—you'll probably have friends for life. Doctors' staffs are on the run as much as waitresses, and high-energy perks can be a boon.

Of course, just because your office is in your home doesn't mean you can't still have coffee and cookies. Goodies are as close as your kitchen. And so are all the other joys of home. After all, isn't that one of the great perks of having a home office?

It is according to the MIB in Denver. She relocated her office from a commercial space to her home so that, she says, "I could be here with my children and keep track of everybody and everything."

Home business office expenses may be deductible. Check out Entrepreneur's *Ultimate Small Business Advisor* for helpful information.

8

Employees, Insurance, and Other Facts of Life

Depending on how much growth you envision for your business, you may never need employees. Or you may expand to the point where you can't do everything yourself. Employees are another of those funny facts of life that seem to bring with them as many cons as pros. When you hire help, you are not a swinging single anymore. You have responsibilities.

▲

Suddenly there's payroll to be met, workers' compensation insurance to be paid, state and federal employee taxes to be paid. And work to be delegated.

Some people are born employers, finding it easy to teach someone else the ropes and then hand over the reins. Others never feel quite comfortable telling someone else what to do or how to do it.

"Up until last month," says the Denver MIB, "I had a staff of about seven. I felt that I had lost control of really doing the work that I love to do, and I was managing people. I grew more than I really felt comfortable growing, so I scaled it back down, and now it's just myself and my 23-year-old daughter. It's just the two of us.

"We've moved back into my home. I did have an office space. I downsized. This is how I want to do it, out of my home so that I can work any time I want to and I can do the work myself instead of managing people all day. I guess I'm a control freak. [I] want to keep control of [the business] and want to know what's going on. And I really enjoy doing the work."

Bright Idea

How about someone from the world of number crunchers, with a background in an accounting office or a bank? They've certainly been trained to cross their ones and dot their twos.

Hired Hands

If you're not fortunate enough to have live-in help, you may want to consider hiring an assistant.

Mary V. and her former partner had one full-time employee, whom they took on after three years in business. This employee did a good portion of their data entry, although she did not come on board with a background in medical billing. "What you need more than anything," Mary explains, "is attention to detail."

Since your assistant will function as an extension of yourself and will represent your business to the outside world, you'll want to choose carefully. A background in data entry or medical billing, or even medical assisting or nursing, is certainly a plus, but just as important—if not more so—is trainability. A person who has no knowledge at all of computers is liable to take an enormous chunk of valuable time to train, but a person who knows computers but not specifically medical billing can be taught to do things exactly the way you want them done.

Organization is a must. So are good telephone skills and the ability to think independently. Your employee will be dealing with clients, insurers, and patients. He or she must be polite, accurate, and assertive. She should be able to bring problems to your attention but also be able to solve problems on her own. If she is constantly interrupting you with questions, you might as well handle everything yourself.

Pay rates for a good data entry clerk run from about $6 to $10 per hour, although this can vary from region to region and on the level of experience. The Walnut Creek MIB pays her employees, all medical billing specialists, $10 and up.

The Backup Brain

Hiring an employee is one of those take-a-deep-breath-or-hyperventilate steps. You're taking on an extension of yourself, someone who with any luck will become not just another pair of hands but a backup brain, a friend, ally, and member of your business family. How do you choose someone to fill all of those shoes?

You want someone with the following skills and abilities:

○ *Analytical skills.* Can they think a problem through and arrive at a solution?

○ *Oral communication skills.* Do they have a good phone personality? Can they communicate a problem? Resolve that problem? Is their vocabulary good? Grammar?

○ *Written communication skills.* Can they write an effective patient or insurance response letter, explaining the problem? Detail the resolution? Communicate grammatically? Punctuate properly?

○ *Detail-oriented.* Can they enter correct codes and patient information without transposing or scrambling?

○ *Able to take direction.* Can they follow directions? And can they do so without getting insulted or defensive?

○ *Personality complements your own.* Some people work better with cheery chatterboxes; others go for the strong, silent type. If you are one and your prospective assistant is another, think twice.

Hours are up to you. You can hire someone to work part time, say, four hours a morning or afternoon or two or three days a week, or you can use your assistant full time, depending on your needs.

Slave Labor

An alternative to hiring an employee is to shanghai an unsuspecting family member. The New Jersey MIB sets her husband to work on occasion while the Denver MIB puts her four daughters, ages 17 to 23, in the computer operator's seat. The eldest is a true employee who's earned the title of bookkeeper; the others fill in here and there. This "helping out" strategy has the advantage of no employee taxes or insurance, although—at least in the case of teens—you'll probably still have to pay your workers. This way, your help is on call 24 hours a day, and you'll know if they're really sick or if they've gone fishin'.

Since much of the data entry can be done at any time, your family crew members can work after school, on a Saturday afternoon, or just about any time that fits into their schedules. Helping Mom or Dad or a spouse with the family business gives everybody a warm fuzzy feeling of pitching in and can be a great togetherness booster.

"And hopefully," the Denver biller says, "they will all take over and then I can retire and just sit back and watch."

Yet another employment alternative is farming out your overload. You can subcontract your data entry work to another billing service and then pay either hourly or per claim. One MIB envisions a time when other people could be routinely set up to do medical billing in their own homes as satellites of his business, thus helping others as he helps himself.

The Temp

Temporary employment services offer the option of employees you can use like library books, borrowing them for the time you need them and then "returning" them with no hard feelings. These employees come prescreened, and all insurance and taxes are covered by the agency. The drawback to the temporary employee is expense.

"I did like the person they sent me very much," the Denver MIB says of her ventures into hiring a temporary bookkeeper and file clerk, "but they're extremely expensive to use. I felt I probably could have gotten someone just as capable by doing a want ad. I probably would have needed to train to some extent, but I wouldn't have had to use that middleman and have the extra expense I incurred."

Insuring Your Gems

Once you find those gems of employees, you'll need to think about caring for them. Workers' compensation insurance laws vary from state to state; check with your insurance agent for details in your area. Workers' comp covers you for any illness or injury that might occur, from a paper cut gone septic to a back injury from lifting heavy file boxes to permanent computer eyestrain. (People can come up with a lot of strange complaints when money's involved.)

Although your employee may be working in your home, your homeowners' insurance might not pay for any such problem on the grounds that it's actually a workers' compensation case.

Rather than making yourself a nervous wreck (incurring your own mental health claim) over all this, check with your insurance agent and then make an informed decision.

"Initially I did the workers' comp month to month," the Walnut Creek MIB says, "because I couldn't afford to pay a whole chunk at a time. They were pretty understanding about that. I worked with ITT Hartford, and they were great. You can do it [that way] when you're in a pinch. I had to have it, but I didn't want to take all my funds and pay a whole year at a time. They worked out a payment arrangement with me. It cost a little bit [in] finance charges, but I think it was only three bucks a month, something like that."

You might want to consider health benefits for your staff. "I provided my staff with health insurance initially and a small life insurance policy," she explains, "and now we have expanded to health, dental, vision, and life insurance."

And they don't even have to handle the paperwork. "The physicians we go to do the claim billing," the former nurse says, "so we're not even involved with that. Which is kind of strange."

The Error of Omitting

Some MIBs are concerned with errors and omissions insurance, which is somewhat similar to malpractice insurance and covers you for nightmarish possibilities such as having a client sue you.

Insurers charge according to risk. Errors and omissions coverage for an MIB business should be about $1,000 to $1,500 per year, but be sure to check with your personal insurance agent for details.

As long as you're worrying at the insurance bone, be sure to update your homeowners' or office rental policy for all your equipment, especially anything new you purchase.

"A lot of insurance companies won't tell you this," the New Jersey MIB confides, "but you can get a nice discount if you send in a videotape [of your office equipment

▲

The Test

O K, your prospective employee looks sharp, sounds professional, and has a nice resume. But how can you know how he'll actually perform once he's on the job? Test him out!

❍ *Write out a typical scenario in which a claim has been denied for a fairly simple reason.* (You be the judge.) You might, for example, use a case in which surgery is shown before the pre-op exam or discharge date before the admission. Ask your prospect to solve the problem.

❍ *Present a scenario of a patient who hasn't paid his bill.* Ask your prospect what he'd say over the phone. Have him type out a letter requesting payment.

❍ *If your prospect is familiar with medical billing, have him enter a claim.* How does he do?

❍ *Have him enter a column of numbers on a calculator.* Does he add it up quickly and correctly?

After you've done all of this for each prospect, you'll want to read resumes, check references, and then use your own people skills. How do you feel intuitively about them?

---

inventory]. I ended up getting a 10-percent break yearly. Any time I buy something, I update that video and take it over to them. Anything happens, I'll get full value."

As with everything else in the MIB business, it pays to get creative. And don't forget that your insurance agent is a great source for new clients!

Forward to the Basics

If you and your computer are starting out from square one, you won't want to concern yourself with insurance policy perks. You can always add these on later when you build a staff and the funds to support them.

Starting out small, or keeping your business small, is in itself a perk, as the Denver MIB found out. She has a 7-year-old son at home, along with her four young daughters. "All he likes to do is turn off the computers," she says. "I haven't taught him anything else right yet. But that's the importance. I think he's the main reason I like to keep it at home—to have him here with me. I love what I do."

Make sure you have the business insurance bases covered: Consider picking up Entrepreneur's *Ultimate Small Business Advisor* for complete information on all small business needs.

Your Operating Theater
Equipping Your Business

Your office will be your operating theater—the dramatic heart of your business—and the proper equipment will contribute greatly to your success. Just as you wouldn't want your neurologist performing brain surgery with a chain saw, so it goes that you won't want to perform delicate electronic operations with a clunker of a computer.

▲

We've provided a handy checklist (see page 137) to help you determine what you will need, what you already have on hand, and which of those in-stock items is MIB-ready. Die-hard shoppers might want to rush out and buy every item brand-spanking new, but this might not be necessary. Some or all of these things might already be meandering around your home, just waiting to be put to use. After you have read this chapter, run through the checklist and evaluate your stock. Is your computer MIB-ready, or is it an antique that won't be able to keep up the pace? Does your answering machine take and receive clearly audible messages, or does it tend to garble crucial information? How about that printer? Can it produce professional looking materials in short order, or does it take ages to spit out a solitary, quavery page? Now, checklist in hand, let's take a whirlwind virtual shopping spree. Ready, steady, go!

Wait a second. Let's discuss something first. There's always the buy of a lifetime and there's always the ultimate fancy-schmancy tip-top of the line. What we're looking for here are the lower-end and middle-of-the-road models.

Computer Glitterati

Your computer will be the star of your office setup, coordinating your billing, accounting, word processing, and desktop publishing activities. In addition to your billing software, it will be arguably your most important purchase. If you already own a computer, you'll want to make sure it's capable of handling the tasks it will be given.

Cybersense

It's easy to get wowed—and wooed—by all the computers at the store vying for your attention. Here's the professional take on what to buy from Margaret, a business machines specialist with Office Depot in Panama City, Florida.

Sit back and take a long, hard look, Margaret counsels, before you purchase a new computer. Her rule of thumb for a small MIB-type business is to consider spending an average of $500 a year on your computer system. For example, if you spend $2,000 on a system (computer, monitor, and printer), you should figure on keeping it for four to five years. If that system helps you make money, she says, then when it comes time to sell, upgrade or give it to the kids, it's lived a useful life.

Margaret also cautions that people tend to overspend. They want to buy the best and brightest but unfortunately frequently end up using only 50 percent of their system's capabilities. She suggests starting out small. "For the entrepreneur or supplemental income [buyer], there's no need to overspend." You can get a good system for around $2,000.

You will want your new computer to have the Windows XP Pro or Vista operating system since this is what new MIB software packages are geared for. To run your medical billing software properly, you'll need at least 512MB RAM, plus at least a 15-20GB hard drive, a DVD-ROM drive and a modem with wireless card, network adapter, and high-speed connection.

You can expect to pay from $2,000 to $4,000 for a good name-brand computer, with prices increasing as you add on goodies.

Monitoring the Monitor

Monitors frequently come as part of the computer package, but they can be bought separately. Make sure you get an SVGA high-resolution color display with a 17-inch screen—large enough to make long-term viewing comfortable.

Keep in mind that as an MIB you'll spend a lot of time in front of that monitor—this is one place where bigger is definitely better. A few extra dollars spent up-front will save hours of squinting in the long haul. If you purchase your monitor separately, you can expect to dish out less than $300 for a 19-inch model.

Flashy Drives

Since data management is the lifeblood of your MIB business, you'll want to back up your files on a daily basis. A flash drive—a small memory stick device—will make these backup chores zip right along. You can always back up the old-fashioned way on disks, but as your databases grow, this becomes an extremely tiresome and lengthy process. Babysitting your computer and popping disks in and out of the drive while it does its thing leaves your hands tied when you could be working on other projects.

Expect to pay less than $25 for a flash drive with 1GB capability or, for backup capability-plus, you can purchase one with 2GB of space for around $35-50.

Purring Printers

A good printer is a must, even though much of your billing will be done online. You'll want to produce reports, charts, graphs, brochures, newsletters, thank-you letters, pay-up-or-else letters, contracts, statements, and sundry other materials, and they all need to look polished and professional. The materials you produce will be a direct reflection on your company. If you still have a dot-matrix printer, ditch it now. Faint, shaky dot-matrix correspondence looks amateurish. Sharp, bold graphics and print give your business an aura of confidence and success.

You also want a printer that's fast. There's nothing quite like the frustration of waiting for material to trickle out of a slow-going printer. One page per minute can seem like one page per hour.

▲

Tip...

Smart Tip

"Grandfather, father and son your backups," Office Depot recommends. This means rotating your backup Zip disks so that you're not copying potentially corrupted files onto already corrupted files. If you rotate, chances are you'll have one set of older, uncorrupted data files.

Fortunately, really hot-stuff printers are much less expensive now than ever before. You can purchase a laser or an inkjet, many of which can produce all the wonderful colors of commercial artwork. Color-capable models print more slowly than their black-and-white colleagues, but if you'll be doing lots of marketing materials like brochures and newsletters, then you'll want to consider color. You can expect to pay as little as $100 to as much as $1,000 for a color inkjet or laser printer suitable for business purposes.

The Fax for You

A fax machine, as we've discussed, is a good way to get raw billing materials from your doctors. But more than that, it makes life much breezier when you want to send or receive certain kinds of information in a flash. For example, you might want to send the insurance carrier a piece of documentation right after you've spoken with them—before they forget what the conversation was about. Ditto for a document to a doctor or patient for clarification. And then, of course, there's that lunch order to the deli down the street.

Fax machines can be purchased as combo fax/copiers, printers, and scanners. They can be very slow when used as a printer, so be sure to check before you buy. Also, make sure the fax machine you purchase will print on plain paper. Expect to pay as little as $100 for a basic plain-paper model and up to $700 for the multifunction jobbies.

Soft on Software

As we've said before, your software is going to be your closest partner after your significant other, so choose carefully. The list of suitors is lengthy, with medical billing/patient accounting programs and packages ranging from $500 to $10,000. Different packages have different capabilities, but more expensive is not necessarily better or worse. You can buy the bare-bones software or purchase a complete business opportunity package, which can include leads generation, seminars, marketing help, and hold-your-hand technical support along with the software.

"You can hire a [local] marketing guru for lots less than [you can buy] a business opportunity," advises Gary Knox of Resource Books, which publishes *The Directory of Medical Management Software*. Don't ignore the business opportunities, he says, but look carefully to make sure you're getting your money's worth.

Whichever option you choose, you'll want to make sure the software is the suitor of your dreams. Here are your dream date must-haves:

- Fields for patient and insurance information
- Ability to establish CPT and ICD-10 databases for your doctors' specialties
- Electronic claims capability
- Paper claims capability
- Posting of payments to patient accounts using open item accounting, which applies payments toward specific charges rather than toward the patient's total balance
- Ability to format and print claim forms and patient statements
- Ability to format patient, provider, insurance company, and other custom lists
- Ability to generate and print reports, including patient ledgers, aging of accounts receivable by patient and insurance carrier, practice analysis (breakdown of charges, income and adjustments for the provider's practice), and other customized reports
- User-friendliness
- Complete documentation
- Readily available coding updates

In addition to all of this, your program-in-shining-armor should be able to perform month-end activities, including:

- Back up data files
- Rebuild data files if needed
- Condense data files as needed
- Recalculate patient balances
- Rebuild all indexes if needed (index files allow you to access data quickly)
- Generate and print month-end reports

Once you identify the software of your dreams and pocketbook, make sure it has a good reputation. Find out how long the vendor or developer has been in business and how many people (preferably thousands) are using the product. Get references, and don't be shy about calling them. Most MIBs are only too happy to share their experiences and will be glad to give you tips other than just a software reference. It can be one of your first forays into networking.

Ask lots of questions. Is the program user-friendly? How good is the technical support? How available is the technical support? How long has the person you're talking to been using the program? Are they happy with it? Have they heard any rumbles about possible problems in the future, such as the vendor leaving for a permanent Tahitian vacation?

Beware!
Many successful billing services have run into rough water when their software vendor went out of business, leaving them with no source for future updates or additional training. Do your homework. Find out all you can.

The Business Opportunity

Shopping for the right software, clearinghouse, or business opportunity is a lot like going on a blind date. You know you're going to have to run through a certain number of nerds before you find the one that makes your heart sing and your computer soar. This is not to say that nine out of ten vendors (and by "vendors" we mean software and business opportunities) are duds. Like other loves in your life, what one person considers perfect may leave another flat.

Here's a sampling of what you can expect to encounter on your search.

- *Lytec Systems.* Lytec sells software only. Its system goes for $1,099 and includes 30 days of toll-free telephone support, after which an additional six months of technical support is available for $449. Lytec offers an interactive training course in which you can learn in the privacy of your own office, using your own data. Lytec is affiliated with Health EDI Services clearinghouse. Because the software and clearinghouse are closely linked, you must use Health EDI (unless you purchase a special module for your computer). Clearinghouse costs are $300 per year in support fees, $50 per doctor and 39 cents per claim.

- *Synergy Medical Information Systems.* A business opportunity vendor in Valparaiso, Indiana, Synergy offers products like medical claims software, CPT and HCPCS, remote access software (so you can work at a client's office or other location in addition to your primary office) and the site licenses you need to use it, Procedure Code Analyzer software, and software to help you learn how to process superbills. The basic Windows-based medical software is $1,795, and a priority service contract (which provides you with technical support for one year) is $995. Its two clearinghouses are fee-free as long they don't have to drop to paper. If they do, they charge 39 cents per claim. According to Tammy Harlan, president, the average amount MIBs spend on the Synergy products needed to get into business is $5,500.

- *USA for Healthclaims.* Another full-service business opportunity vendor located in Audubon, New Jersey. In addition to helping you with many of the same services you have read about in this guide, USA provides Windows-

Beware!
Is a business opportunity seller doing the hustle? Watch out for a salesperson who says things like "Territories are going fast." Legitimate sellers will not pressure you to rush into a big decision. If someone does, just say no.

based electronic claims filing software, classroom training, and a presentation video that can be shown to prospective clients. Contact the company directly for costs (see Appendix A).

Clearinghouse Check-Up

Before you decide on a clearinghouse, don your mental detective garb and investigate. Make sure you find the answers to the following:

- Which payers is the system connected to? Does it handle all major commercial payers? How about HMOs, the Blues, Medicare, and Medicaid?
- How many payers does it connect to? The more it hooks up with, the less additional work for you.
- Can you rely on it to accommodate all payer reporting requirements?
- How many medical practices and billing services does it count as clients? A large number here is a good indicator that the service is tops.
- Does the clearinghouse return claim audit information to you in the form of

> **⚠ Beware!**
> Not all business opportunities are the same. One might consist of as little as a start-up manual; another will provide you with software, in-depth training, and ongoing sales, marketing, and technical support. It is your responsibility—a big one—to find out exactly what you're buying. Don't make the assumption that because one offers a particular service or feature, another one will, too.

(Don't) Fly Me to the Moon

Because medical billing is such a hot field, it is unfortunately open to scam artists. In other words, business opportunity vendors who will cheerfully take your money, hand over some software and disappear into the void. No support, no follow-up, no trail. No good.

Do your homework! Find out everything you can about the vendor's history and reputation. Check references. Check with your local Better Business Bureau to see if any complaints have been filed. Check with your state attorney general's office. You should also check with the BBBs and attorneys general in surrounding areas or states (scammers like to stay on the move).

You know—if you've been following along in this book—that the MIB business is not a ticket to overnight success. If a vendor promises you'll make oodles of money in your first year, take a hint: Go with someone else. In most states, promising the moon is not only unethical but downright illegal.

reports? How long does it take to receive information? Some return information in a few minutes, some in 24 hours, others in a few days.

- Does the clearinghouse offer value-added services to help improve your productivity, such as electronic remittance advisories, electronic funds transfers, or suspense files? (The latter bumps back to you for review of any weirdies such as a patient marked "female" but named "John.")
- What equipment, software, and training will you need?
- What kind of ongoing support is offered? This is a biggie. Since payers frequently change the score card, buying each other out and potentially changing data requirements, the system must be periodically updated.
- What's the track record for support and maintenance? How fast will the clearinghouse respond if you have a problem?
- References? Ask for names and phone numbers of current clients and then do your homework. Check them out. If any are near you, ask if you can drop by and see the system in action.
- How long has the clearinghouse been in business? Check around for any rumors of disbanding or dissatisfaction.
- Are the system and software fully functional? Purchasing a system under development can spell trouble.
- Can the system accommodate your billing software?
- What's the per-claim cost?
- Is there an annual fee?
- Is there a per-doctor fee?
- Will it send paper claims to payers that aren't EDI-capable? This is another biggie. If it does, it streamlines your work considerably.
- Who has access to the data you submit? What security safeguards are in place to protect confidential information?

You can expect to pay from zero to $300 in clearinghouse initiation fees. In addition, some clearinghouses may charge a per-doctor fee of about $50.

More Software

A dazzling array of software lines the shelves of most office supply stores, ready to help you perform every business task—design and print your own checks, develop professional-quality marketing materials, make mailing lists and labels, be your own attorney and accountant.

Most new computers come preloaded with all the software you'll need for basic office procedures. If yours doesn't or if you've lucked into a stripped-down hand-me-down, you might want to look into the following programs. You should have a word

Step Into My Office

Office furniture is another optional item. It's important that your work environment is comfortable and ergonomic, but if you're homebased, it's perfectly acceptable to start off with an old door set on cinder blocks for a desk and an milk crate for your files. When you're ready to go the big step toward real office furniture for that oh-so-professional look, you have a stunning array of possibilities to choose from.

We shopped the big office-supply warehouse stores and found midrange desks from $200 to $300; a computer work center for $200; printer stands from $50 to $75; two-drawer, letter-size file cabinets (which can double as your printer stand) from $25 to $100; and a four-shelf bookcase for $70.

Chairs are a very personal matter. Some people like the dainty secretary's chair for its economy of space; others want the tonier high-back executive model. There are chairs with kangaroo pockets and chairs with pneumatic height adjustments. Prices range from $60 to $250.

processing program to write correspondence, contracts, reports to go with the charts from your billing software, and whatever else strikes your fancy. You can find a good basic program such as Microsoft Word (the business industry standard) for $230 or Corel WordPerfect Office X3 for around $300.

You might also want an accounting program such as Intuit's QuickBooks or Microsoft Money to track your business finances. These are a sort of checkbook on a CD-ROM and make record-keeping a breeze. You assign categories such as office supplies and business travel to the checks you write, and at tax time, you print out a report showing how much money you spent for what. Your accountant not only will thank you but will charge you less for not having to wade through all your receipts. You can expect to pay from $49 to $250 for your cyberspace checkbook.

You'll want a desktop publishing program for those polished marketing materials. Try Broderbund's Print Shop Pro Publisher Deluxe for around $100 or Microsoft Publisher for $170. Both are

Bright Idea

Purchase a greeting card program. You can customize not only the artwork, but the text or verse and matching envelope. Sending a personalized thank-you card, with the addressee's name embedded right in the message, makes a terrific impression. You can find professional quality (and really fun!) greeting card programs in the $30 to $50 range.

▲

very user-friendly and can be used to create a bevy of marketing materials from business cards and brochures to banners and signage. A nice complement is Photoshop Elements from Adobe, a slimmed-down version of the big daddy of photography/design softwares, Photoshop. For about $100, you get most major elements of the straight-up version, but with more flexibility and ease of use. It's a great graphics programs for beginners.

Hello, Central

You will probably have three telephone lines coming into your home, two of which will be for your office. Therefore, you will want a two-line phone so you can put one on hold while you are answering the other line. You can divide up the three lines any way you like: You might put your home line and your business line on the two-line phone, leaving the third line for your fax machine and modem. Or you might put the business and fax-modem line on the two-line phone, leaving your home line in the kitchen or den. Perhaps you wish to use a mobile phone as your main office number, freeing up the land line for faxes. The idea behind these choices is that you can call out on your home or fax-modem line (when it's not in use) and leave the business line for incoming calls.

Fun Fact

On the medical time line, the WHO, developer of the ICD codes, came up with the codes in 1893 as a formalization of the Bertillon Classification or International List of Causes of Death. The acronym ICD is a vestige of the codes' original title.

A speaker is also a nice feature, especially for all those on-hold-forever calls to insurance carriers. Your hands are free to enter data, your shoulder remains unhunched, and there's no earring jabbing you in the back of the head while you listen to Muzak and wait your turn.

You can expect to pay about $70 to $150 for a two-line speakerphone with auto redial, memory dial, flashing lights, mute button, and other assorted goodies.

Automated Answering Service

Since you'll probably be out of the office at least part of every week, picking up billing materials and calling on clients, you'll need a receptionist—and it will probably be automated. If you choose not to go with voice mail from your local phone company, your "secretary" will be an answering machine.

The models on the market now are digital, which, aside from the technical mumbo jumbo, means that they don't have audiotapes to get knotted or broken. There are also all sorts of fancy gizmos complete with caller ID, speakerphones, cordless phones, and 15 kinds of memos, but a good basic model capable of answering your business line can be had for less than $40. For a snazzier cordless phone model that can answer two lines, expect to pay about $150.

Vociferous Voice Mail

⚠ **Beware!**
Remember that coding books are updated annually. Make sure the version you have on hand is the most recent.

Voice mail is the phone company's answer to the answering machine, with a few nice twists. Like an answering machine, voice mail takes your messages when you're not in the office. If you have call waiting, a feature that discreetly beeps to announce an incoming call while you're already on the phone, and you choose not to answer that second call, voice mail will take a message for you. Lots of other fun features, such as your very own voice-mail hell ("If you want information on X, press 2"), are also available in various parts of the country.

Voice-mail costs depend on your local phone company and the features you choose, but you can expect to pay around $6 a month for basic service.

Rah-Rah Reference Manuals

Your library should contain those runaway bestsellers, *Current Procedural Terminology*, otherwise known as the CPT, and *International Classification of Diseases, Revision 10*, aka *ICD-10*. You'll also want the hit pick of the medical set, the *HCPCS (HCFA Common Procedure Code System)*. If you're going to be filing dental claims, definitely add *Current Dental Terminology*, aka *CDT 2007-2008*, published by the American Dental Association.

The Ingenix people (formerly Medicode) offer great versions of these manuals (excluding dental), geared toward individual specialties or as a complete listing, in text versions with punchy graphics on the covers, either online or CD-ROM. Prices vary depending on what you buy, but as an example, you can get the EndcoderPro package on CD-ROM that contains all the CPT, ICD-10-CM and HCPCS codes for less than $300.

There are a variety of other sources for coding books out there. For example, Unicor Medical offers their *Easy Coder* series of ICD-9 books for individual specialties. So, if you are doing billing for, say, a chiropractor, you can score an *Easy Coder* book just for that purpose. These quick-reference specialty books run around $62.

You should also check out Ingenix's *Insurance Directory*, which gives addresses and phone and fax numbers for scads of carriers. It also uses fun icons to identify which types of claims the carrier pays (e.g., optical or dental), which carriers accept electronic claims and which accept HCPCS codes on the commercial claims. You can expect to pay about $80 for this gem.

▲

Form-Fitting

Because of the red ink involved, you'll need to purchase CMS 1500 forms. (The form is only considered "official" when it's the preprinted version done in jazzy red ink.) These forms come imprinted or plain, on plain or continuous feed paper, two-part or one-part, with sensor (bar code) or without, in boxes of 1,500 to 3,000. You should allocate $35 to $100 per box.

Laugh at Lightning

You should invest in a UPS, or uninterruptible power supply, for your computer system, especially if you live in an area where lightning or power surges are frequent occurrences. If you're a computer newbie, you may not realize that even a flicker of power loss can shut down your computer, causing it to forget all the data you've carefully entered during your current work session or—the ultimate horror—fry your computer's brains entirely. With a UPS in your arsenal, you won't lose power to your system when the house power fails or flickers. Instead, the unit flashes red and sounds a warning, giving you ample time to safely shut down your computer.

Read All About It!

The written word is a powerful learning tool. One of your first steps in your new venture should be to read everything you can, not just about the specifics of medical billing, but about starting a small business and marketing and sales techniques. Blitz the bookstore. Make an assault on your public library.

Your own business library should contain more than your coding manuals. You'll have the documentation that comes with your software or business opportunity package and your Medicare Guides, but you should also check out the following:

○ *The Ultimate Small Business Advisor* (Entrepreneur Press), by Andi Axman
○ *The Guerrilla Marketing Handbook* (Houghton Mifflin Co.), by Jay Conrad Levinson and Seth Godin
○ *Understanding Health Insurance, A Guide to Professional Billing* (Delmar Publishers), by JoAnn C. Rowell

Don't stop with these. Immerse yourself in your subject. The more you know, the better MIB you'll be. Read all about it!

Since you'll be working online quite a bit, you want to be sure that your UPS includes phone line protection. You can expect to pay $125 and up for one of these power pals.

Lightning Strikes Again

A surge protector safeguards your electronic equipment from power spikes during storms or outages. Your UPS will double as a surge protector for your computer hard drive, or CPU, and monitor, but you will want protection for those other valuable office allies—your printer, fax machine and copier. They don't need a UPS because no data will be lost if the power goes out, and a surge protector will do the job for a lot less money. If you have a fax machine, be sure the surge protector also defends its phone line. You can expect to pay in the range of $15 to $60.

Smart Tip

Bar-coded forms, used to track claims, are required by some carriers and frowned upon by others. Make sure you find out the drill in your area before you order.

Cool and Calculating

What do calculators and telephones have in common? A numbered keypad and an important place on your desk. Although your MIB software will do the patient accounting calculations for you, there are always spur of the moment arithmetic questions you can answer more quickly without having to zip around through cyberspace. And with the paper tape, you can check your work. Expect to pay $15 to $25 for a battery-operated model and $25 to $50 for a plug-in job. A full-size adding machine is about $100.

Bright Idea

If you plan to generate a lot of paper claims, you might want to look into a postage meter. This is a time saver in the lick-and-stick department, the standing-in-line-at-the-post-office department, and, with those envelope sealing gizmos, they can even protect against those pesky paper cuts.

Paper Cloning

The copier is an optional item, probably the least important on the list, but as you grow, you may find it a necessary luxury. Keep in mind that you should never send a piece of paper out of your office unless you've kept a copy. Copiers may cost $500 and up, while the toner cartridges they consume sell for around $10 to $15 each.

Equipment Expenses

To give you an idea of how much you can expect to budget, check out the cost of furniture, equipment, and supplies for two hypothetical medical billing services, Medical Claims Plus and Quality Computerized Claims. Medical Claims Plus, a homebased newbie with no employees except its owner, has monthly gross collections of $900. The fledgling business counts as its equipment resources an inexpensive computer system, an inkjet printer, and the basics in software and reference materials.

Quality Computerized Claims, up and running for three years, make its base in an office in a medical complex, has one full-time employee in addition to the owner, and has monthly gross collections of $12,000. Quality Computerized Claims boasts a top-of-the-line computer system for its owner, an inexpensive computer for its employee, a laser printer, a combo fax machine/scanner, a copier, various reference books, and publishing and marketing software that have caught its owner's eye over the years.

Furniture, Equipment, & Supplies	Medical Claims Plus	Quality Computerized Claims
Computer system (including printer)	$2,000.00	$4,000.00
Fax machine	100.00	700.00
Billing software/business opportunity	700.00	5,000.00
Clearinghouse	300.00	N/A
Other software	350.00	500.00
Phone system	70.00	160.00
Answering machine	40.00	130.00
Reference manuals	200.00	400.00
Uninterruptible power supply	125.00	250.00
Flash drive backup	50.00	50.00
Surge protector	34.00	34.00
Calculator	15.00	50.00
Copier	N/A	700.00
Desk	200.00	600.00
Desk chair	60.00	200.00
Printer stand	N/A	70.00
File cabinet	25.00	200.00
Bookcase	70.00	70.00
Computer/copier paper	25.00	50.00
Blank business cards	6.00	12.00
Letterhead paper	30.00	30.00
Matching envelopes	35.00	35.00
10 x 13 envelopes	14.00	28.00
Legal-sized envelopes	3.00	6.00
Address stamp or stickers	10.00	10.00
Extra printer cartridge	25.00	80.00
Extra fax cartridge	N/A	80.00
Zip drive disks	45.00	120.00
Mouse pad	10.00	20.00
Miscellaneous office supplies	100.00	150.00
Total Expenditures	**$4,642.00**	**$13,735.00**

The MIB Office Checklist

Use this handy list as a shopping guide for equipping your office. It's been designed with the one-person home office in mind. If you have partners or employees or you just inherited a million dollars from a mysterious foundation with the stipulation that you spend at least half on office equipment, you might want to make modifications.

After you have done your shopping, fill in the purchase price next to each item, add up the total, and you'll have a head-start on the "Start-up Expenses Worksheet" on page 103.

❑ Windows XP or Vista-based Pentium PC with
SVGA monitor, modem, and DVD-ROM drive $_____

❑ Laser or inkjet printer   _____

❑ Fax machine   _____

❑ Business/marketing software: _____
    Word processing   _____
    Desktop publishing   _____
    Accounting   _____

❑ Phones, two to three lines with voice mail, or
answering machine   _____

❑ Uninterruptible power supply   _____

❑ Flash drive   _____

❑ Surge protector   _____

❑ Calculator   _____

❑ Computer/copier/fax paper   _____

❑ Blank business cards   _____

❑ Blank letterhead stationery   _____

❑ Matching envelopes   _____

❑ 10 x 13 envelopes   _____

❑ Legal-sized envelopes for mailing claims   _____

❑ Return address self-stamper or stickers   _____

❑ Extra printer cartridge   _____

❑ Extra fax cartridge   _____

❑ Zip drive disks   _____

❑ Mouse pad   _____

❑ Miscellaneous office supplies (pencils, paper clips, etc.)   _____

Not on the Critical List

❑ Copier   _____

❑ Desk   _____

❑ Desk chair   _____

❑ Filing cabinet   _____

❑ Bookcase   _____

Total Office Equipment and Furniture Expenditures $_____

Blowing Your
Own Horn

OK, you've passed Medical Insurance 101 with flying colors. You've done your market research, figured out your finances, and persuaded your family to act as in-a-pinch employees. Now you need clients.

As we've often stressed, landing that first client can be the hardest part of the medical billing business. But there are ways to nab that first doctor, and the one after that, and the one after that.

The absolute best way to attract clients is through word-of-mouth. Doctors have a set of jungle drums, a grapevine. Doctors gossip. Like that shampoo commercial where the silken-tressed model tells two friends and "they tell two friends and they tell two friends," doctors also pass the word on. The New Jersey MIB can attest to this. Once she got her first client, she says, "It rolled from there."

"Yeah," you might be muttering aloud, "but how do I get the first one?"

Relax. You have a lot of options.

People Will Talk

The first option is referrals, or networking, which is really a variation on word-of-mouth. The difference is that with word-of-mouth, you sit back and wait for others to talk about you and send business your way. With networking, you actively seek referrals.

Talk to everybody that you know. Let them all in on the exciting news that you're now running a medical billing service. You can start with your own doctor. Next time you see her on a professional basis, tell her about your service. But don't ask directly for her business, as this might put a strain on your relationship.

Chances are, however, that she'll have referrals and probably some tips on how to approach other doctors. Terrific! It's always easier to call other doctors when you can say "Dr. Whatsit suggested I call," or "Dr. Whatsit referred me." People always pay more attention when someone they know has given you the green light.

After you talk to your doctor, call other providers you know directly or indirectly: your children's pediatrician, your husband's internist, your father's cardiologist, your pharmacist and dentist. Using the name of a recognized patient, or being one, can give you a foot in the door.

Once you've tapped out those resources, start approaching physicians who specialize in an area you're interested in. For instance, if you have small children, you might start with pediatricians; if you're into athletics, you could try sports medicine practitioners.

There also are lots of other people you already know who you can put on your networking list. Your attorney, accountant,

> ## Smart Tip
>
> *Tip...*
>
> "I think the biggest fear of people who are getting into this business is how they're going to market themselves," Kim H. offers. "My advice to them is make yourself well-known at first and then when you get that first client, just really work hard and get that money in. Do a really good job, and it's like it just goes from there."

insurance agent, and real estate agent probably have their own little card files full of physicians and will be happy to make referrals. (After all, you are their client. They want to keep you happy. Besides, most people like helping a fellow businessperson.)

Remember how Kim H. in Virginia went to see her local hospital administrator? He referred her to her first two clients. This is something you can try yourself.

When you're finished with professional types, call your friends. Call your parents. Call your parents' friends. There's nothing parental units like better than helping out some nice young person (no matter what age you feel you are). Can you imagine a motherly type not calling her pal—whose son/cousin/in-law is a doctor—with the news that her best friend Sylvia's daughter is starting a medical billing business and is looking for clients? Of course she will, and you should take advantage of that. Good referrals can come from unlikely sources. And everybody either knows somebody or knows *somebody* who knows somebody. This is what makes networking work.

The MIB Letter

Many MIBs have had great success with newsletters or other direct-mail pieces.

"I really think my newsletter did it," the New Jersey MIB says triumphantly. "That got me the two psychologists right off the bat." She also did a few "walk-ins," which netted her another psychologist, who referred her to a psychiatrist.

Along with the newsletter, New Jersey's first mailing included an introductory letter and a sort of resume describing her services.

She now sends out a newsletter to existing clients about every two months, featuring small articles about coding changes—and more. "With mental health, it's good," she says, "because there's so many ways a psychologist who's not bringing in many insurance patients [can increase his income]. He could be making money other ways—by volunteering [his] time at the courthouse, by networking with attorneys."

This is a good strategy for any potential client newsletter. When you show doctors your expertise in various phases of medical billing or practice management, you give them the confidence to go with your company. You can also make their mouths water. Let them think "Wow, if I had this billing service, I'd have this sort of stuff available all the time."

"I don't gear it just toward billing," the New Jersey biller explains. "I gear it toward other things that they're going to be interested in. I keep them pretty happy with that."

The San Diego MIB landed her first client through a direct-mail survey, which included a cost analysis. But it wasn't a quick sale.

> **Fun Fact**
>
> According to the National Center for Health Statistics, women visited the doctor's office two times more than men in the 18-44 age group. Why the increase in visits? This group is of childbearing age.

▲

"I worked with the office for about five months before actually signing them," the former nurse says. "I really had to build a good rapport with [the receptionist] because she's the one who answers the phone. I have to go through her to get to the office manager, and I have to go through the office manager before I can get to the doctor. Becoming a friend and ally [with the front office people] is the best thing you can do."

> ### Bright Idea
> If you have pre-MIB credentials that will reflect positively on your business, such as an RN or a history with an insurance carrier or large billing company, make sure you mention it in your newsletter. Use your history to your advantage!

Summer vacations and the likelihood of the office manager going on disability contributed to major holdups in the doctor's decision-making process. "During that time I had to be very patient, very businesslike, and understanding that they weren't just putting me off," the San Diego MIB recalls. "I could have thought 'Oh, you know, they're just putting me off and they don't really want to do this.' And they could have just fallen through the cracks, but I was persistent and stayed with them. And always, before I got off the phone with them, I made a follow-up appointment. So it wasn't like we hung up the phone and I didn't have a guaranteed connection with them again."

Persistence paid off. She landed the doctor and is now doing full-practice management for him.

In her survey, she came up with several questions designed to custom-tailor her sales pitch for each doctor she approached.

She asks how much the target office knows about electronic billing so that she can go into the right amount of detail when she makes her in-person pitch. She asks what their claims volume is and what it's costing them to send claims on paper. Another question focuses on which carriers are billed and at what percentage.

"Those are the main things," she says. "And then one of the last things I ask is what their specialty is, how many doctors they have and how many years they've been in practice."

She averaged a 20 percent return from this mailing, which is a very good response. Look at it this way. If you mail out a similar survey to 100 doctors and net a 20 percent return, that's 20 doctors who have more or less given you an invitation to call on them.

At 'Em Advertising

More traditional forms of advertising such as print ads, TV or radio spots, and Yellow Page ads don't seem to do as well for the MIB as the methods we've just discussed: cold calling, calling-all-relatives, networking, and direct mail.

"Advertising, I think, is a waste," Mary V. says bluntly.

"I did do a box ad in the Yellow Pages," says the Denver biller. "I don't really feel that for the price I paid over the year, I got any business from it, so I went back to just a line listing in the Yellow Pages."

This is not to say that a phone company ad won't work for you. If you decide to give the Yellow Pages a shot, go for a box ad. Not only do these stand out from the rest—they also lend an impression of greater professionalism. Be sure you mention in your ad your specialties and other services that might benefit the client.

Smart Tip Tip...

Most medical billing services advertise under the heading "Billing." Some advertise under "Insurance" or "Insurance Services" and some under "Medical and Dental Business Administration." Find out what the norm is in your area, then go with one or more of the above.

If you can get your local Yellow Pages to give you a good rate, an ad couldn't hurt. But you might do better to concentrate your advertising and marketing budget on direct mail. You'll already have a computer. With the desktop publishing programs that are available now, you can afford to experiment. Write up ad copy, pop in some clip art. Have fun with it.

Direct Mail Dazzle II

Use the letter on page 145 for your direct-mail ad campaign. You can use it as is by retyping it onto your letterhead, or you can modify it in any manner that feels right to you, but keep in mind the following:

❍ Try writing as if you were speaking to a friend. You want your letter to sound professional, of course, but stiff and stodgy doesn't create interest. Keep it peppy!

❍ Don't be modest. List by name all industry associations to which you belong and any certifications you have.

❍ Don't forget to insert your cost analysis! You can use the survey from Chapter 4 as a template or design your own.

❍ Remember that SASE (self-addressed stamped envelope)!

❍ Check to make sure you've spelled the doctor's name and business name correctly!

❍ Make sure everything else is spelled correctly and your grammar and punctuation are fine-tuned.

❍ Remember to stick to the point. Don't let your words wander.

▲

Bright Idea

Use your clip art to spark ideas. "In one [mailing] I have," the San Diego biller says, "there's clip art with a little guy with several different hats on, and I'm appealing to the office manager or the doctor, whoever it is that wears many hats in the office."

The San Diego MIB—the one who netted her first client with a survey—has been having a ball with her two desktop publishing programs.

"It's fun," she says. "I'm not a very creative person by nature. It takes a lot of work for me to produce something creatively. When somebody gives me an idea, then I can [say] 'Oh!' It gives me ideas of how to go about it. These templates are great. You just pick the different clip art and then if you want it arranged [differently], then you just change a few things and it's done. I love doing desktop publishing now."

Direct mail is inexpensive compared with some other forms of advertising. When you consider that, aside from your time, your only expenses are stationery and stamps, what have you got to lose? Or to turn it around, what do you have to gain?

(Cold) Calling All Clients

If you hated the "ask the fellow" part of Sadie Hawkins dances, or if you were at the bottom of the Cub Scout candy-sales pack because you didn't like knocking on doors, then cold-calling (calling on a prospect unannounced) will leave you chilled to the bone.

Although general industry reviews are mixed, the MIBs we talked with who have tried this approach were pleased with the results. "What [the business opportunity vendor] said, which I thought made sense," Curt J. says, "is if you don't have any clients yet and you don't have any experience, the only thing you have to sell is yourself. So because I wasn't afraid of face-to-face selling, I just made up my own brochures along with some other material, and I went door to door and gave them my materials. I followed up with another visit and then followed that up with a phone call."

The Montana MIB got her first two clients through cold-calling. "I made personal contacts," she says. "I created some quality hand-outs and reply cards, and I do my own personal contacts [by walking] into doctors' offices and leaving information."

The Doctor's World

Calling on doctors is a unique experience. They usually have a chorus line of patients waiting in the wings, colleagues and pharmacists dialing up with questions, and assistants darting back and forth with questions from patients. There's little time for dillydallying, shooting the breeze, or kicking back for a cup of coffee and a chat. If you understand how a doctor's office works, you'll have a better chance of seamlessly insinuating yourself into it.

Old Oak Claims Services

345 Main Street
Huckleberry, New Hampshire 00001
Phone (000) 000-3456
Fax (000) 000-3457

June 12, 20xx

Dr. Wally Whatsit
123 North South Street
Huckleberry, NH 00001

Dear Dr. Whatsit:

How would you like to have your patients' bills paid—on time, hassle-free, and without you or your staff having to lift a finger?

Sound like a dream? It's not. And I'm the person who can make it a reality. My company, Old Oak Claims Services, is in business for the sole purpose of taking insurance claim nightmares and patient billing headaches out of your office, leaving you and your staff free to do what you do best—practice medicine.

My services range from claims filing to full-practice management. I pry your money out of insurance companies. I know how to get claims paid quickly, and I know what to do if a problem arises. I don't get paid until you do, so my incentive is strong. I can also provide you with the best in patient accounting, from posting and mailing bills to full accounts receivable operations. I can provide you with reports customized for your practice, giving you fingertip information on every aspect of your collections.

I stay abreast of the latest in health-care changes and challenges, just as you do, through ongoing education. I attend seminars given by Medicare, Blue Cross/Blue Shield, and other insurers. Through my membership in industry associations, I have access to the best and brightest industry tips and techniques.

I know I can increase your collections! I'd like to show you how. Simply fill out the enclosed cost analysis and fax it to me at (000) 000-3457. Or pop it in the mail in the enclosed self-addressed stamped envelope.

I look forward to talking with you and your staff and tailoring a program for you. Feel free to call me with any questions at (000) 000-3456.

Best regards,

Judy January

Judy January
Old Oak Claims Services

P.S. For a limited time, I am offering a free month of Medicare billing. Why? To show you that I'm serious about saving you money. And that I know once you see how hassle-free your collections can be, you'll be hooked!

As with most businesses, the typical health-care office is made up of various personalities, job descriptions, and educational backgrounds. The staff usually includes a receptionist, various office assistants, an office manager and clinical staff help such as nurses, therapists, or hygienists. Let's look at this motley crew to find out who does what:

- *Receptionist.* This person's responsibilities vary according to the size of the practice. In a large office, the receptionist may simply answer the phone, but in most practices, she (or he) is also responsible for scheduling appointments, collecting patient information, taking messages, and opening and routing office mail.

- *Office assistants.* Large medical and dental practices employ office assistants to help the receptionist with clerical and administrative tasks such as maintaining patient accounts and general bookkeeping. They may or may not have a say in administrative decisions, but it's a smart idea to deal with them as if they do.

- *Office manager.* If the physician's practice is large enough to have an office manager, this person is usually responsible for managing the office staff, maintaining patient relations, monitoring accounts and collections, gathering financial information for the doctor and accountant, and overseeing office operations. The doctor usually grants the office manager a great deal of decision-making power. She might have been trained at a trade school and might have several years' experience in health-care administration. Winning over this key staffer can be every bit as important as winning over the doctor. If you succeed in gaining her interest, she should have enough leverage to set up the big meeting between you and her boss, and the doctor will take her suggestions seriously. In some cases, the office manager has the authority to decide on her own whether to use your service.

- *Clinical help.* Nurses, therapists, hygienists, and other medical assistants usually work in the back office. They assist the doctor with clinical work and usually have little input when it comes to business decisions.

Handle with Care

Because the medical billing industry took off with such a bang, many doctors got burned by MIBs who didn't know the ropes. Business opportunity vendors pulling people off the street put a lot of people in the driver's seat who really didn't belong there. Consequently, a lot of doctors got dinged with heavy fines and even the threat of losing their Medicare billing status. This has, not surprisingly, turned them MIB-shy.

More and more doctors are now receptive to outsourcing, but to some extent they're still skeptical because they've been stung by people who didn't know what they were doing.

This is yet another reason continuing education on your part is vitally important. When you point out to potential clients that you really do know your business, that you belong to industry associations and attend classes and seminars on an ongoing basis, your credibility—and your salability—will rise.

In fact, staying current with insurance issues and regulations like HIPAA are key to success in this industry, according to Tammy Harlan, president of Santiago SDS Inc., a medical billing business opportunity vendor in LaPorte, Indiana.

"Training boosts your confidence," says Harlan, who is a former MIB herself. "It also helps you keep up with the changes and complexities of this industry, which makes you more valuable to your clients."

Capture That Client

Once you have a doctor sit down and listen to your pitch, how do you close the sale? One way is by sitting on his chest until he yells "OK!" and signs on the dotted line.

Getting Past the Gatekeeper

In most offices, the doctor is protected from the outside world by a bevy of staffers who have been trained to guard him with their professional lives. These gatekeepers feel it's their job to fend off callers—phone and in-person—so the doctor can do his job uninterrupted.

Getting in to see the doctor without bleeding, sneezing, or limping can sometimes seem an insurmountable task, like breezing in to see the pope on your way through Vatican City.

"For the most part," Curt J. says, "I found three kinds of offices. There were those that, as soon as [the office staff] found out what you were doing, felt threatened or intimidated. A couple commented 'You want my job.' I tried to assure them that's not why I was there." This type of office, he found, represented the minority of those he visited.

The second type was ruled by the office manager. "Getting to them was fairly simple and easy, even if there was a receptionist," Curt says. Of the third category, he says, "Regardless of how big the staff is, the doctor pretty much has his finger in every arena and operation. If that's the case, I was able to get to him fairly easily also."

The Montana biller also found that approaching the doctor was often a cinch. "Many times, the doctors would be there in the area and I would actually visit with them," she says. "It makes it much more personal. They're the ones who are going to make the decision."

This is not recommended. The preferred method is to offer him options he can't refuse. You can offer to bill him on a per-claim basis, hourly, or on a monthly percentage basis.

Percentage Pow!

Let the doctor know that when he pays you a percentage of his collections, you both come out winners. The San Diego MIB pitched her provider this way: "I'd be charging on a percentage of claims, but [your] overhead would come way down."

Obviously, it was a winning pitch because she's now doing full-practice management for him. It worked because she told him he couldn't lose. He'd gain not only in increased collections but also in reduced overhead. He could afford to send his former office manager off on disability because he'd be replacing her with an outsource service for which he did not have to pay hourly wages, workers' compensation insurance fees, or payroll taxes.

The Denver MIB explains her rationale for charging on a percentage basis this way: She says it's her incentive to make sure things are done correctly and that she collects on the claims. "If we don't collect, the doctor doesn't get money, and neither do we."

This is an excellent bargaining table technique. Everyone understands the desire to make money. Put it to the doctor in these same terms; it tells him that you're going to work hard because you want to see cash pile up. When you combine this technique with the facts of lowered overhead and increased collections, you have a hard-to-ignore sales pitch.

The Per-Claim Pitch

You can pitch the per-claim basis by showing the doctor that it costs less to pay you so much per claim than it does to pay an in-house staffer to do the same thing. When you figure in payroll costs and the costs of paper, software, and clearinghouse fees and compare it with your per-claim price, you have a great sales technique.

Use this data as a starting point:

- The cost per claim for a paper claim can reach $18-25, compared with just $1.50 to $3 for an electronic claim, according to the American Medical Association.
- Less than 1 percent of first-time electronic claims are rejected. They're also paid within 7 to 21 days, vs. 90 to 120 days for paper claims.
- Doctors can reduce outstanding accounts receivables by more than 60 percent by using electronic claims submission.

Home in on your closing. Point out that your expertise will net the doctor more collected claims. Explain that when you do the claims, that's all you do. Your attention won't be diverted by other demands of a busy office. You're free to concentrate on making sure the claims get paid. His staff is free to take care of patients, and no one needs to worry about follow-up because you'll do it all.

You Must Remember This

Don't undersell yourself. Once you've locked yourself into a contract, you're stuck for the duration. There's nothing like the rocks-in-the-pit-of-the-stomach feeling of signing a client only to discover that that great low, low price you've negotiated won't pay for the time it takes to do the work. Plus, if you've negotiated high enough, when contract renewal time rolls around, you'll meet less resistance with the same fee structure than if you try to bump up your rates.

Don't be discouraged if you don't close the sale on your first meeting. As long as the doctor doesn't bark out a flat "No!" the door is still open. Even if he does say no, you can always go back in a few months and see if things in his office—or in his mind—have changed. Just make sure you set up an opportunity for another phone call or visit before you leave the office.

Let the doctor help with negotiations. Ask what she needs and wants. Ask what it would take to have her sign with your service.

Curt J. signed his first clients on a per-claim basis, doing electronic filing of claims he entered on his own software. He was very upfront when he started the working relationships. "I told them, 'The reason I am doing this is because I want all your

Smart Tip

Tip...

Save your hourly basis pitch for offices where the other two methods of pricing just won't work; for example, a provider who sees few patients. Pitch this fee structure the same way you'd pitch per-claim and percentage bases. It's still a good deal for the doctor and still a good deal for you.

Forms for Lunch

Along with the contract, work out other details with the doctor and his staff, such as who will handle calls to and from patients regarding their insurance claims and the charges they owe and what you expect the office to provide when you pick up information: superbills, reports, or EOBs you'll need to send with claims, new patient fact sheets and new insurance information.

You might design a handy checklist for the office to use each time they prepare a folder full of goodies for you or a packet containing materials such as precertification and predetermination forms. All of this is great PR!

business someday,'" says the former pastor/MIB. "'But I am willing to start doing it this way: a) because you need it, but b) at some point in time you're going to have to upgrade your office. At that point in time, I'm hoping to get all your business.'"

People Who Need People

Here's another excellent technique. Telling the client that you want his business may sound redundant, but it's not. Everybody wants to be wanted (except by the IRS). Everybody wants to feel important. When you bring this into the open, you're telling your prospect that you think enough of him and his business to strive for it. People respond in kind.

A good way to get your potential client to work with you in negotiations is by asking open-ended questions. You want to know the "reporter's six:" what, where, when, why, how, and who. For example, who in the office does the billing currently, how long does it take, when does it get done, etc.? Asking these sorts of questions as opposed to close-ended questions that can be answered with a short 'yes' or 'no' gets the prospect talking and thinking and gives you the opportunity to respond.

Be creative. If you meet with opposition, think of ways around it. You might, for example, offer a free month's trial service or a waived setup charge. Curt gave a prospective client three free months of Medicare filing and then immediately wowed her with claims paid in record time. His strategy is simple but elegant: After three months of such service, she'll be hooked. Not signing a contract to continue his service will seem insane.

Putting out a Contract

Once you've convinced the doctor that you can handle his work, it's time to put it in writing in the form of a contract. This is where you establish exactly what each of you will provide the other. Spell out how often you'll pick up information from the office, how often you'll send patient statements, what types of reports you'll generate, and at what intervals (once a month, once a quarter).

You'll also need to cover your fee, how often you'll bill the doctor, and when you expect payment. Be sure that you cover termination of the contract, specifying who has the right to terminate it and how much notice they need to give. You should also specify for how long you expect to be paid after you've stopped billing.

You can use the sample "Health-Care Billing Agreement" on page 152 as is or modify it in any way you choose. After you've fine-tuned it, however, seek a second opinion. "Any agreement," the San Diego biller advises, "should be looked at by an attorney before having a client sign it, to make sure all bases are covered."

When you give free trial service, you're doing three things. One, you're showing the doctor that you have faith in your operations; therefore, they must be good. Two, the learning curve is a freebie, too. If you discover after the trial noncontracted period that you hate the MIB business, you can bow out gracefully. (But of course, you won't.) Three, it lands that first elusive client. After the first one, word-of-mouth and your own increased confidence will carry you along toward more sales.

One Singular Sensation

How you present yourself at a sales presentation is as important as how you present your business. Even if you're doing the actual billing in your blue jeans, you need to show up at your prospective client's office dressed for success. Wear business apparel. Make sure your shoes and briefcase or handbag are clean and/or polished. Check before you leave home to ensure that all sales materials—your business cards, brochures, and any charts or peripheral goodies—are clean, tidy, and organized.

It's a good idea to call ahead to confirm the appointment. Doctors can get tied up with an emergency or a waiting room full of anxious patients. When you arrive, arrive on time. If you're late, you're sending a message that you don't value the doctor's time and that you're not efficient, the exact opposite of the message you want to convey.

It's only natural to be nervous. Don't let it throw you. Doctors are used to people who aren't at their best. They're not expecting you to tap dance into the office with a top hat and cane. (Although that does make a lasting impression.)

Remember that you know what you're talking about. Have faith in yourself, your service, and your abilities. Believe it or not, your confidence will come through. You needn't imagine the doctor stark naked, as professional lecturers sometimes do of their audiences, but do picture him as an equal. He's a professional at his job; you're a professional at yours.

Public Relations Patter

Once you land your first clients, you should continue to promote yourself to them and to new prospects with public relations. The newsletters we've already discussed are excellent PR tools. Through them, you keep your existing clients abreast of new rules and ideas and, with luck, get them to brag about you to their colleagues. When they use the tips you provide, they help you become more efficient. Newsletters also tell your clients that you're still thinking of them even though you already have the contract and that you're always working toward increasing their collections. This helps get your name circulating on the doctor grapevine and also ensures that the doctors you have sign on for another year when renewal comes up.

Health-Care Billing Agreement

This agreement is made by and between _____ (hereinafter called "Billing Service") located in _____ and _____ (hereinafter called "Provider") located in _____, _____ on this _____ day of _____, .

Whereas, Billing Service provides services to health-care providers designed to effectuate the filing of medical insurance claims with governmental authorities and private commercial carriers through electronic and manual means (Claims Processing) and also offers direct billing services to the patient (Billing Services); and

Whereas, Provider desires to engage Billing Service to provide Claims Processing and/or Billing Services as set forth herein.

Therefore, Billing Service and Provider agree as follows:

1. Billing Service Responsibilities:

A. *Claims Processing.* Billing Service will pick up claims information from Provider every _____, unless other arrangements have been made and both parties have agreed. Billing Service will file, process, and collect Provider's claims and provide a computer-generated report verifying their receipt by the insurance companies on a _____ _____ basis. The claims will be processed within _____ business days, excluding those that contain errors made by the Provider's office, unless alternate arrangements have been made and both parties have agreed.

B. *Billing Services.* Billing Service will bill patients for services rendered by Provider on a schedule of _____.

2. Provider Responsibilities:

A. *Claims Processing.* Provider agrees to provide certain information regarding patients and their insurance coverage that is necessary to enable Billing Service to file and process medical insurance claims. Billing Service shall not be responsible for any delay in or ability to collect claims due to insufficient information provided by Provider.

B. *Billing Services.* Provider agrees to submit in a timely manner all necessary billing information to enable Billing Service to bill patients in the time frame required by the Provider.

Health-Care Billing Agreement, continued

3. Provider's Payment of Services:

A. *Claims Processing.* Provider agrees to pay Billing Service the sum of $___ _____ per insurance claim filed and processed, or at the rate of _____ percent of the total dollar value of all collections.

B. *Billing Services.* Provider agrees to pay Billing Service the sum of $___ _____ per billing prepared and sent to patient, or at the rate of _____ percent of the total dollar value of all patient statements collected.

C. Billing Service reserves the right to change the rate of compensation upon submission of thirty (30) days' written notice to Provider.

D. In the event that a claim or billing must be resubmitted due to an error by Billing Service, the same shall be resubmitted at no additional cost to Provider.

E. In the event that a claim or billing must be resubmitted without fault on the part of Billing Service, the same shall be resubmitted by Billing Service and Provider agrees to pay Billing Service the charge set forth herein as if such resubmission were an original submission.

F. Billing Service will provide a month-end invoice with all charges due, with attached monthly reports. Remittance of these charges will be due in full within 10 days. Late payments are subject to a 2-percent late fee and accounts over 45 days are subject to suspension of services unless prior arrangements have been agreed upon in writing.

4. Designation of Billing Service as Provider's Authorized Agent:

Provider hereby appoints and designates Billing Service as its agent for the limited purpose of billing and corresponding with insurers regarding processing and collection of insurance claims, and any insurer or payer of claims is authorized in its dealings with Billing Service as the Agent of Provider for this limited purpose.

5. Relationship of the Parties:

Billing Service and its employees and contractors shall at all times be independent contractors and not employees of Provider. Billing Service shall not have any authority to compromise claims or to otherwise bind Provider except as expressly set forth above, and Provider shall have no authority to bind Billing Service.

▲

Health-Care Billing Agreement, continued

6. Term of Agreement:

A. This Agreement shall be in effect for one (1) year from the date of execution.

B. Either party may terminate this Agreement at any time, with or without cause, by giving thirty (30) days' written notice of termination to the other party. Upon termination of service, Provider agrees to immediately remit to Billing Service all charges and fees owed to date.

7. Confidentiality:

A. Billing Service agrees and covenants to keep all information concerning physician and its patients, including personal and financial information, strictly confidential, and Billing Service agrees that it will not disclose any such information to any person or third party except as may be reasonably necessary to file and process claims and/or patient billing.

B. Provider agrees and covenants to keep all information concerning Billing Service and its fees strictly confidential; and Provider agrees that it will not disclose any such information to any person or third party except as may be reasonably necessary or with prior consent of Billing Service.

C. The foregoing provisions regarding confidentiality shall survive the termination of the Agreement. Furthermore, the foregoing provisions constitute independent covenants and shall not be discharged by any breach or default of the party seeking their enforcement.

8. Warranty:

Billing Service's warranty under this Agreement shall be limited to the rerunning, at its expense, of any inaccurate reports or forms, provided that Provider furnishes verification of the inaccuracy of any such report or form, and provided further that such inaccuracies were caused solely as a result of Billing Service's performance, and provided further that Billing Service shall receive written notice of such inaccuracies within ten (10) days of delivery of the inaccurate materials. Provider agrees that the foregoing constitutes its exclusive available remedy.

9. Limitation of Liability:

A. Provider agrees that the foregoing warranty is in lieu of all other warranties, expressed or implied. Provider further agrees to maintain copies of all patient information supplied to Billing Service so that at no time will Billing Service possess data that is not simultaneously maintained in Provider's own office.

B. Billing Service has no liability to Provider if data or records are destroyed by fire, theft, acts of God, or any other cause. In the event of system malfunction, for whatever reason, or inability to access the computer, Billing Service shall not be liable for damage to or loss of any Provider data that has been entered into the computer system. However, Billing Service will use its best efforts to minimize the possibility of such damage to or loss of Provider data by use of regular backup procedures.

C. Provider agrees to hold Billing Service harmless from liability resulting from violations of state or federal laws or regulations relating to the extension of credit or handling of accounts receivable by Provider. Provider agrees to aid in the defense of Billing Service in any such state or federal proceeding.

The parties hereto have executed this Agreement as of the day and year set forth above.

Provider

By:_____

Billing Service

By:_____

Overture, Curtains, Lights!

The house lights glow, the orchestra warms up, an eager murmur fills the room. OK, scratch the orchestra and replace it with subtle mood music on your CD player. Then go with the excitement. It's your grand opening!

Invite doctors and staffers to whom you've sent out surveys, newsletters, and introductions as well as those you've called. Invite your friends and family for moral support. Send an invitation to the local press, explaining your service and why it benefits patients as well as physicians.

Besides libations, have brochures, business cards, and sample charts and reports on hand. Make up something your guests can take away with them:

- ○ A set of patient appointment cards with your business name printed on the bottom or back
- ○ A set of patient birthday cards with your business name printed on the back
- ○ A set of notepaper with your business name printed at the top. All of these can easily be generated with your desktop publishing program. Or, you can go with the following:
  - − A stack of precertification forms with your business name printed across the top
  - − A stack of predetermination forms with your business name printed across the top

You can use materials from your newsletters to publish articles in local medical association publications or to give talks for the same associations. You can also pull out promotional material from your brochures.

How about going on the air? Volunteer yourself for a local radio station's chat show. You can use your same materials for discussion. Listeners can call in and ask questions, then tell their doctor they talked to you. If you do a little research to discover which stations doctors and their staff listen to in the office, for instance, you'll get even more of the exposure you want.

If you're aware of a promotional event in town where you think doctors might show up—say, a charity function or golf tournament—offer to help. If the event will aid an environmental cause, you can point out that your services are green—by filing electronically, you use fewer paper products, thus saving trees. The main benefit you'll get from attending these events is that you can meet doctors, shake their hands, and be a familiar face to them. Then, when you call on them, you have a common ground. You can say "Remember me? We met at the Save the Spotted Owl Charity Ball."

Are You Being Served?

Since your clients will be signing a contract, repeat business will not be the problem it can be for a retail company. You still, however, need to be concerned with customer service. An unhappy client will not sign on for another year and will not refer other providers, which, as you know, is where you'll get a great deal of your new business.

The best way to handle your clients is the way the Denver MIB does. "They all feel like they're my only client," she says.

Make sure your doctor and his staff feel important, well cared for and in good hands. Return phone calls promptly. Follow up on questions. If you don't know the answer to something, find it. When the Illinois MIB is posed a problem he doesn't readily know how to solve, he doesn't hem and haw. He's honest. He tells his clients, "I'm not really sure; I want to be really exact when I talk to you. Let me find out and get back to you on that."

Kill Them with Kindness

Treat patients the same way you treat the doctor and her staff. Patients will report back to the office on your behavior and your problem-solving abilities. The best way to get an "A" is to make them feel special, too. But sometimes this can be difficult. Patients can be impatient, cantankerous, and cranky, especially when they get a bill they don't understand. How do you respond in such a case?

"Kill them with kindness," the Denver MIB counsels. "It makes them angrier, actually, but at least you feel better when you get off the phone. That's something that I have always, always drilled into any bookkeepers who have worked for me. You don't give back to them what they're giving to you. That makes no sense, and you just end up in a catfight. There's no production in that.

"If they want to blow off to you, that's fine because you know that it's not [personal]. As long as your information is correct, you know that, yeah, they're angry, they've got a big bill. They're having problems with the insurance company, they can't get it figured out, and you're the person they've called and were able to talk to."

This is the key. To the patients, you're accessible. You're someone to whom they can vent their frustration. Don't take it to heart. But don't be a doormat, either.

"I do not tolerate extreme rudeness," the Denver biller says. "I do not tolerate any kind of vulgarities. If they really want to yell at me, I usually will say, 'If you can calm down and talk nicely to me, courteously to me, then we can get this resolved and I'll

▲

Fun Fact

Joseph P. Kennedy, financier and patriarch of the famous Kennedy clan, is said to have made a point of picturing important personages with whom he was negotiating in their red flannel underwear.

---

help you out any way I can. If you can't, then we'll terminate this conversation and I'll just write you a letter.' I really am willing to do whatever to help. And I have avenues that I can [use to] help that they don't have. It needs to be a team effort.

"The bottom line is, if they just continue to be rude, I just let them know, 'I'll just send you a letter recapping what we've talked about, and I'll let the doctor know about our conversation. And if there's anything I can do to help, give me a call.' And I'll terminate the conversation. I won't be yelled at. So long as we can keep our calm, then at least there's some semblance of order, and we get things done."

More Pain Management

Controlling Your Finances

Whether you are a chronic number cruncher or one of the finance-phobic, you'll want to give your company periodic financial checkups. "Why?" you ask. "I already did all that math stuff in the start-up chapter." That was the prenatal exam for the precious baby that's your business. When you've gone through the birthing process and that precocious tot is toddling around, you'll want well-child checkups to make sure your business is as healthy as you imagine.

If there is a problem, you will find out before it becomes critical. For example, if you discover that your per-claim charge barely covers your expenses, you can quickly change gears and raise your price or fee basis before signing another client at the same too-low rate. You can also take measures such as switching to a less expensive clearinghouse, cutting back on mailings, or axing those gorgeous but expensive 6-color brochures from the printer in favor of those banged out on your own printer.

Financial checkups don't have to be negative. They can give you a rosy glow by demonstrating how well you are doing—possibly even better than you expected. If you have been saving for a new printer or software program, or if you are hoping to take on an employee, you can judge how close you are to achieving that goal.

Tracking your percentage of collected claims will also give your success rate. If it's high, you can use it to convince new providers to come on in—the water's fine. If it's lower than you thought, now's the time to re-evaluate your billing techniques and make the necessary changes.

Making a Statement

An *income statement* (also called a *profit and loss statement*) charts the collections and operating costs of your business over a specific period of time, usually a month. Check out the income statements on pages 164 and 165 made for two hypothetical medical billing services, Acme and Zephyr. Acme is a newbie, just starting out with one client, while Zephyr, which has been up and running for two years, is breezing along with four clients. Although Acme bills per claim and Zephyr takes a percentage of fees collected, they both cast their income statements the same way.

Acme processes 300 claims per month and charges $3 per claim. Zephyr collects an average of $40,000 per client each month from which a 7 percent commission is deducted. Acme, a one-woman band, is owner-operated and has its home base in the guest bedroom. Zephyr has one full-time employee and makes its base in a downtown office. Neither owner draws a salary; they both rely on a percentage of the net profit for their income.

You will notice that several expense categories have been left blank. We have listed them so you can get an idea of what you might want to use in your income statement. Feel free to tailor your statement to your particular business. If you don't have these categories, leave them out.

To make your statement really right, you need to prorate items that are paid annually, such as business licenses, tax-time accounting fees, or clearinghouse annual fees, and pop those figures into your monthly statement. For example, if you pay a clearinghouse annual "membership" fee of $300, divide this figure by 12 and add the resulting $25 to your clearinghouse expense. This will bump up your monthly clearinghouse expense of, say, $120, to $145, but it will also give you an accurate picture of what your costs are throughout the year.

Use the worksheet on page 166 to chart your own income statement. You'll be surprised how much fun finances can be!

Dud Doctors

You may encounter a situation in which you have plenty of clients to net a profit, your collections are humming along and yet your income is low. You've run into the Case of the Dud Doctor, the one who can't seem to pay his account with you. This is not a frequent problem in the medical billing world, but it does happen.

Kim H. faced this difficulty with one of her first clients. "The money he was getting in he was spending rather than paying his bills," she explains. The root of the problem went beyond the doctor himself. "When I went through my training, they said you have to watch physicians' wives and see how closely they're involved in the business. That's a real true statement, because the wife got involved and felt that the claims weren't coming in fast enough, so they wouldn't pay me." In essence, the claims were coming in rapidly, but the doctor and his wife used slow reimbursement as an excuse for not coughing up the fees.

Kim handled the situation in a professional manner, deftly lobbing the problem into the doctor's court. "We talked about it," she explains. "At first I went and said, 'I really don't think it's a good idea; maybe we should terminate our contract,' and that I would stay with him [until] he could find somebody else, but things worked out. He's paying me, and his money's coming in, and he's getting his financial situation straightened out.

"That was a biggie," she adds with some relief. "That was probably [the] only major problem that I've ever had."

The Walnut Creek biller, with 10 years of experience and more than 50 physicians to her credit, encounters few payment problems. "They are all very honorable people," she says of her clients. Of her creed, "Pay the bill in a timely manner or we stop doing [your] work," she adds, "I've had people test me a little bit to find out if I really will, and when they find out I really do, then they're fine."

For more payment collection tips as well as other good information, check out Entrepreneur's *Ultimate Small Business Advisor*.

> **Tip...**
>
> **Smart Tip**
> Send your monthly invoice along with your monthly report of how much you've billed—and collected—for your provider. The invoice won't hurt him as much when he can immediately compare it with the report. Plus, it gets your bill noticed quickly!

▲

The Tax Man Cometh

Just as into each life a little rain must fall, so from each business a little tax must be paid. If your budget allows, you should also engage an accountant. You probably won't need her for your daily or monthly concerns, but it's well worth the expense to have someone in the know holding the reins when it comes to April 15, or for those rare Panicsville questions that come up now and again.

Your tax deductions should be about the same as those for any other small or home-based business. You can deduct a percentage of your home office so long as you're using it solely as an office. These deductions include all normal office expenses plus interest, taxes, insurance, and depreciation (this is where the accountant comes in handy). The IRS has added in all sorts of permutations; for example, that the total amount of the deduction is limited by the gross income you derive from the business activity minus all of your other business expenses apart from those related to the home office. And you thought that new board game you got for Christmas had complicated rules!

Basically, the IRS doesn't want you to come up with so many home office deductions that you end up paying no taxes at all. If, after reading all the lowdown, you're still confused, consult your accountant.

What else can you deduct?

- Business-related phone calls
- The cost of business equipment and supplies (again, so long as you're truly using them solely for your business)
- Subscriptions to professional and trade journals

> **Smart Tip** *Tip...*
>
> If your local community You can call the IRS with questions at convenient 800 numbers all over the country. You might have to go through Voice Mail Hell and a lengthy hold period, but once you get a live being on the line, he or she will be surprisingly friendly.

> **⚠ Beware!**
>
> Although the IRS allows attendance at conventions, they've apparently watched too many episodes of The Love Boat. They draw the line at conventions held on cruise ships.

• Auto expenses: These accrue when you drive your trusty vehicle in the course of doing business or seeking business. In other words, you're chalking up deductible mileage when you motor out to your clients' offices to pick up superbills or day sheets, or when you take a spin to Dr. Whosit's office to make a sales presentation.

It's wise to keep a log of your business miles. You can buy one of several varieties at your local office-supply or stationers store, or you can make one yourself. Keep track as you go. It's no fun to have to backtrack at tax time and guesstimate how many miles you drove to how many clients how many times during the year.

Smart Tip

The IRS loves documentation. The more receipts and logs you accumulate and carefully organize, the happier you'll be if the "A" word (audit) rears its ugly head. The more documentation the better. The IRS can disallow anything without it.

- *Entertainment expenses.* Think wining and dining Dr. Whatsit during the course of a sales pitch or hosting Dr. Whosit's staff at a coffee hour. Keep a log of all these expenses as well, especially if they come to less than $75 a pop (you don't technically need to keep receipts for these), and if you're entertaining at home, have your clients or prospects sign a guest book.

  You must have a business-related purpose for entertaining, such as a sales presentation or a Q&A session. General goodwill toward your fellow medical professionals doesn't cut it, so be sure your log contains the reason for the partying.

- *Travel for business purposes.* If you attend a seminar or train with your business opportunity vendor, you can deduct air fares, bus tickets, rental car mileage, and the like.

- *Hotels and meals.* Since the IRS allows deductions for any such trip you take to expand your awareness and expertise in your field of business, it makes sense to take advantage of any conferences or seminars that you can attend.

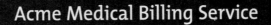

Acme Medical Billing Service

Income Statement
for the month of June 20xx

Income

Monthly collections	$900.00	
Gross Monthly Profit		$900.00

Expenses

Clearinghouse fees	$120.00	
Rent		
Phone/utilities	25.00	
Postage/delivery	10.00	
Licenses/taxes		
Employees		
Benefits/taxes		
Ad/promo	100.00	
Legal services		
Accounting services		
Office supplies	20.00	
Maintenance		
Transportation	15.00	
Insurance		
Subscriptions/dues	8.00	
Miscellaneous	50.00	
Total Monthly Expenses		$348.00

Net Monthly Profit   **$552.00**

Zephyr Medical Billing Service

Income Statement
for the month of June 20xx

Income

Monthly collections	$11,200.00	
Gross Monthly Profit		$11,200.00

Expenses

Clearinghouse fees	$480.00	
Rent	500.00	
Phone/utilities	400.00	
Postage/delivery	300.00	
Licenses/taxes		
Employees	1,750.00	
Benefits/taxes	350.00	
Ad/promo	500.00	
Legal services		
Accounting services		
Office supplies	40.00	
Maintenance		
Transportation	25.00	
Insurance	90.00	
Subscriptions/dues	8.00	
Miscellaneous	50.00	
Total Monthly Expenses		$4,493.00

Net Monthly Profit | | **$6,707.00**

Income Statement Worksheet

For the month of _____

Income

Monthly collections	$_____
Gross Monthly Profit	$_____

Expenses

Clearinghouse fees	$_____
Rent	_____
Phone/utilities	_____
Postage/delivery	_____
Licenses/taxes	_____
Employees	_____
Benefits/taxes	_____
Ad/promo	_____
Legal services	_____
Accounting services	_____
Office supplies	_____
Maintenance	_____
Transportation	_____
Insurance	_____
Subscriptions/dues	_____
Miscellaneous	_____
Total Monthly Expenses	$_____
Net Monthly Profit	$_____

12

Operating Successfully or Pulling the Plug

Most people succeed in the medical billing field by following the tried and true business methods of persistence and plain old-fashioned hard work, with a healthy dose of optimism liberally sprinkled throughout. If we've illustrated anything in this book, we hope it's that becoming an MIB involves

Tip...

Smart Tip

Keep your company growth factor at a comfortable level. "I'm not out for quantity," says the biller in Denver. "I'm out for quality. I'm only taking on accounts when I know that the ones I now have are running smoothly. I'm not for [just] numbers because then you start losing."

a lot of work. It's rewarding and sometimes exhilarating work, but it's darn hard work nonetheless.

We also hope we've managed to convey that becoming an MIB is not the same as becoming an overnight success. It takes a lot of knocking on doors to achieve that first client and more knocking to land the ones that follow.

Ground Zero

When the MIBs interviewed for this book were asked what they would do differently if they could start over from ground zero, they gave—not surprisingly—some very honest responses.

"I would plan for more hours," the Illinois MIB says. "The marketing end was definitely more time-consuming than I originally scheduled."

Time was also a concern for the Montana biller, who was holding down a full-time job as a bookkeeper while she was landing and then billing for her first clients. "I felt I couldn't put as much into it as I would have liked in the beginning," she says. She also admits, however, that being able to work at outside employment while starting a new business is an advantage—you still have to buy groceries. Wearing two hats was the hardest part, but she's quick to add, "I'm still glad that I've done it the way I've done it."

"I would be more careful about how fast I grew," the Denver biller says. "At one point I grew too fast, and I started to feel like I was losing control of things, and [the clients] couldn't get the personalized service. So I would be very careful about growth and make sure that I did not shortchange any of my physicians."

The teacher, Kim H. in Virginia, attributes much of her success to having chosen the right business opportunity vendor, one she feels comfortable with and one who offers a lot of support. "I'm being honest about this," she says. "Things have gone really good and really smooth."

The Quality of Life

At some point during your business's first year of life, you will want to run a happiness checklist. Are you operating successfully? Is your quality of life fulfilling? Or should you pull the plug?

Whether or not you're earning money, the success of your business is contingent on a happiness factor. Because it is a lot of work and a lot of responsibility, you might discover that you'd be just as happy—or even more so—working for someone else. With everything you will have learned, you'll be a great job candidate.

None of the people interviewed for this book seem to have any intention of packing it in. The Montana MIB seemed to mirror the thoughts of all when she said she's excited about having her own business despite the hard work. "You're putting into it as much as you can to be able to have the advantages later on," she says.

Bright Idea

Start a local MIB support group. The San Diego MIB found kindred souls in her area on the internet and through referrals from her business opportunity. These fellow MIBs have become friends and mentors. She plans to meld them into a group that meets once a month or more to discuss common goals and problems.

She also doesn't let cold-calling faze her. Rather, she gives it the Schwab's Drug Store approach, like a movie star on the verge of discovery. "It's surprising how you have to be at the right place at the right time," she says, "but that's all it takes."

Likewise, the biller in San Diego refuses to be bothered by the competition. There is some competition in her area, she says, but there are more than enough doctors. "Every billing center can't be everywhere; there's plenty of business to be had," she contends.

These seem to be the attitudes of all the MIBs who so generously helped with this book. Winning attitudes. If you go into the business with the right stuff—a willingness to work hard and to learn everything you can; the confidence to promote yourself and your business; and the drive to succeed—chances are you will.

Appendix A
Medical Claims Billing Resources

They say you can never be rich enough or young enough. While these could be argued, we believe "You can never have enough resources." Therefore, we present for your consideration a wealth of sources for you to check into, check out, and harness for your own personal information blitz.

These sources are tidbits, ideas to get you started on your research. They are by no means the only sources out there and they should not be taken as the Ultimate Answer. We have done our research, but businesses—like patients—do tend to move, change, fold, and expand. As we have repeatedly stressed, do your homework. Get out and start investigating.

As an additional tidbit to get you going, we strongly suggest the following: If you haven't yet joined the internet age, do it! Surfing the internet is like waltzing through a vast library, with a breathtaking array of resources literally at your fingertips.

Associations

American Association of Healthcare Administrative Management, 11240 Waples Mill Road, #200, Fairfax, VA 22030, (703) 281-4043, fax (703) 359-7562, www.aaham.org

American Dental Association, 211 E. Chicago Ave., Chicago, IL 60611, (312) 440-2500, www.ada.org

American Medical Association, 515 N. State St., Chicago, IL 60610, (800) 621-8335, www.ama-assn.org

Blue Cross and Blue Shield Association, 225 N. Michigan Ave., Chicago, IL 60601-7680, (312) 297-6000, www.bluecares.com

National Electronic Billers Alliance, 2226-A Westborough Blvd., #504, South San Francisco, CA 94080, (650) 359-4419, fax (650) 989-6727, www.nebazone.com, e-mail: merry@nebazone.com

(*Note:* Just about every medical specialty has a professional organization, which you can find by calling a specializing physician or by checking the internet.)

Books

The Guerrilla Marketing Handbook, Jay Conrad Levinson and Seth Godin, Houghton Mifflin Co. (and any other *Guerrilla Marketing* books—all terrific!)

The Ultimate Small Business Advisor (comes with spreadsheet CD-ROM), Andi Axman, Entrepreneur Press

Understanding Health Insurance, A Guide to Professional Billing (comes with practice CD-ROM), JoAnn C. Rowell, Thomson Delmar Learning

Business Opportunities

See Entrepreneur's BizOppZone Web site at www.entrepreneur.com/bizoppzone

Clearinghouses

ET&T (Electronic Translations and Transmittals Corp.), 4838 E. Baseline Road, #118, Mesa, AZ 85206, (800) 950-3868, (480) 325-0901, fax (480) 325-0902, www.ettch .com

AIS Compliance, Atlantic Information Services Inc., (a company that provides special-ized business information for health-care managers) 1100 17th St. NW, #300, Washington, DC 20036, (202) 775-9008, (800) 521-4323, www.aishealth.com, e-mail: customerserv@aispub.com

American Hospital Association, One North Franklin, Chicago, IL 60606-3421, (312) 422-3000, www.aha.org

Centers for Medicare and Medicaid Services, 7500 Security Blvd., Baltimore, MD 21244-1850, (410) 786-3000, www.cms.hhs.gov

HIPPAAdvisory (sponsored by Phoenix Health Systems and a provider of HIPAA knowledge and solution), www.hipaadvisory.com

HIPAAcomply (an online source for HIPAA security and privacy compliance information), Beacon Partners Inc., www.hipaacomply.com

U.S. Department of Health and Human Services, 200 Independence Ave. SW, Washington, DC 20201, (877) 696-6775, (202) 619-0257, www.hhs.gov

Mailing Lists

Lytec Systems Inc., 5222 E. Baseline Rd., #101, Gilbert, AZ 85234, (800) 735-1991, www.lytec.com

Medisoft, 5222 E. Baseline Rd., #101, Gilbert, AZ 85234, (800) 333-4747 for sales, (800) 334-4006 for support, www.medisoft.com

Medical Claims Software/Clearinghouses

Lytec Systems Inc., 5222 E. Baseline Rd., #101, Gilbert, AZ 85234, (800) 735-1991, www.lytec.com

Synergy Medical Information Systems, 1150 Eastport Drive, Suite C1, Valparaiso, IN 46383, (800) 652-3500, fax (219) 531-7540, www.santiagosds.com

USA for Healthclaims Inc., 39 E. Kings Hwy., Audubon, NJ 08106, (800) 809-0670, (856) 415-9453, www.usaforhealthclaims.com

Medicare

Highmark Medicare Services, www.highmarkmedicareservices.com (Although the HGS people handle Medicare for the state of Pennsylvania and fee-for-service Part A for Pennsylvania, Maryland, and District of Columbia, their Web site contains lots of information of interest and value to anybody in the health insurance field.)

Medicare Handbook, U.S. Government Printing Office, 732 N. Capitol Street NW, Washington, DC 20401, (866) 512-1800, (202) 512-1800 (DC area), http://book store.gpo.gov

▲

Newsletters

Coding News, Unicor Medical Inc., 4160 Carmichael Rd., Montgomery, AL 36106, (800) 825-7421, fax (800) 305-8030, www.unicormed.com

The Electronic Biller Newsletter, Electronic Medical Billing Network of America, Inc., 51 Eton Court, Bedminster, NJ 07921, (908) 470-4100, fax (908) 470-4233, e-mail: merl@medicalbillingnetwork.com

Healthcare Billing and Management Association Newsletter, Healthcare Billing and Management Association, 1540 South Coast Highway, Suite 203, Laguna Beach, CA 92651, (877) 640-HBMA (4262) Ex: 203, fax (949) 376-3456, www.hbma.org

Online Postage

Pitney Bowes, www.pitneybowes.com

USPS, www.usps.com

Professional Journals

Medical Economics Magazine, 123 Tice Blvd., Suite 300, Woodcliff Lake, NJ 07677, (201) 690-5300

Reference Books

American Dental Association, Catalog Sales, (800) 947-4746, www.ada.org

American Medical Association, Catalog Sales, 515 N. State St., Chicago, IL 60610, (312) 464-5000, (800) 621-8335, www.ama-assn.org

INGENIX, (800) INGENIX, www.shopingenix.com

PMIC (Practice Management Information Corp.), 4727 Wilshire Blvd., #300, Los Angeles, CA 90010, (800) MED-SHOP, fax (800) 633-6556, www.pmiconline.com

Unicor Medical Inc., 4160 Carmichael Rd., Montgomery, AL 36106, (800) 825-7421, fax (800) 305-8030, www.unicormed.com

Seminars

American Society of Plastic Surgeons, 444 E. Algonquin Rd., Arlington Heights, IL 60005, (888) 475-2784, www.plasticsurgery.org

McVey Associates Inc., 150 Ford Way, Suite 100, Novato, CA 94945, (800) 227-7888, www.mcvey seminars.com

Southern Medical Association, 35 W. Lakeshore Drive, Birmingham, AL 35209, (800) 423-4992, www.sma.org

(*Note:* Check with the professional organizations for the specialties you'll be billing to see if they schedule seminars.)

Successful Medical Billing Services

Account Resolutions LLC, Mary J. Vandegrift, 8775-P Cloudleap Ct., PMB 46, Columbia, MD 21045, (443) 259-0660, e-mail: maryvande@aol.com

Medical Billing Systems of Rockford, Curt Johnson, P.O. Box 4782, Rockford, IL 61110, (815) 226-0669

Quality Billing Services, Kim Hooker, Route 2, Box 119, Lebanon, VA 24266, (540) 889-2411

Appendix B

Medical Claims Forms

▲

HIPAA Business Associate Agreement

This is a sample recommended by AHIMA

Contractual Agreement

This agreement is made effective as of [date], by and between [client and client address] and [contractor and contractor address]. In this Agreement, the party who is contracting to receive services shall be referred to as [client acronym], and the party who will be providing the services shall be referred to as [contractor acronym].

The parties agree as follows:

Description of Services: Commencing [date], [contractor] will provide the following services (collectively, the "Services"):

(Spell out specific services, any required due dates, and any required outcome measures, such as:

1. review policies, procedures, and systems relative to health information privacy and security for compliance with federal and state law and regulation and standards of practice

2. review policies, procedures and systems relative to electronic signatures for compliance with federal and state law and regulation and standards of practice

3. provide a written assessment identifying any shortcomings or opportunities for improvement and suggested methodologies for bringing existing practice into compliance with federal and state law or existing standards of practice)

Performance of Services: The manner in which the Services are to be performed and the specific hours to be worked by [contractor] shall be determined by [contractor]. [Client] will rely on [contractor] to work as many hours as may be reasonably necessary to fulfill [contractor's] obligations under this agreement.

Price and Payment Terms: [Client] will pay a fee to [contractor] for the Services in the amount of [dollar amount]. This fee shall be payable [method of payment, i.e., in a lump sum upon completion of the service, based on an hourly rate billed at the end of the month and payable within 30 days]. Upon termination of this Agreement, payments under this paragraph shall cease, however, [contractor] shall be entitled to payments for periods or partial periods that accrued prior to the date of termination and for which [contractor] has not yet been paid.

Term/Termination: This Agreement shall terminate automatically upon completion by [contractor] of the Services required by this Agreement. Either party may terminate this agreement with or without cause by submitting a 30-day written notice.

Relationship of Parties: It is understood by the parties that [contractor] is an independent contractor and not an employee of [client]. [Client] will not provide fringe benefits, including health insurance, holidays, paid vacation, or any other employee benefit, for the benefit of [contractor].

Confidentiality: [Contractor] recognizes that [client] has patient health information and other proprietary information (collectively, "Information") which are valuable, special, and unique assets of [client]. [Contractor] will not divulge, disclose, or communicate in any manner any Information to any third party without prior written consent. [Contractor] will protect the Information and treat it as strictly confidential. [Contractor] will abide by the requirements of 42 CFR, Part 164.506, Standards for Privacy of Individually Identifiable Health Information: Proposed Rule. A violation of this paragraph shall be a material violation of this agreement.

Legal Fees and Court Costs: In the event any legal action is taken to enforce this agreement or any portion thereof, the party that prevails in that suit shall be entitled to recover from the other, reasonable attorney fees plus the cost of said suit.

Notices: All notices required or permitted under this Agreement shall be in writing and shall be deemed delivered when delivered in person or deposited in the United States mail, postage prepaid, addressed as follows:

[Client Contact Name and Address]

[Contractor Contact Name and Address]

Such address may be changed from time to time by either party by providing written notice to the other in the manner set forth above.

Entire Agreement: This Agreement contains the entire agreement of the parties and there are no other promises or conditions in any other agreement whether oral or written. This Agreement supersedes any prior written or oral agreements between the parties.

▲

HIPAA Business Associate Agreement, continued

Amendment: This Agreement may be modified or amended if the amendment is made in writing and is signed by both parties.

Severability: If any provision of this Agreement shall be held to be invalid or unenforceable for any reason, the remaining provisions shall continue to be valid and enforceable. If a court finds that any provision of this Agreement is invalid or unenforceable, but that by limiting such provision, it would be come valid and enforceable, then such provision shall be deemed to be written, construed, and enforced as so limited.

Waiver of Contractual Right: The failure of either party to enforce any provision of this Agreement shall not be construed as a waiver or limitation of that party's right to subsequently enforce and compel strict compliance with every provision of this Agreement.

Applicable Law: This Agreement shall be governed by the laws of the State of [state].

Signature Party Receiving Service _____

Signature Party Providing Service_____

Form provided courtesy of the Medical Association of Billers, www.e-medbill.com

HIPAA Authorization Form

This form is recommended by the AMA.

Authorization for Use or Disclosure of Information for Purposes Requested by Physician's Office

_____

I, _____, hereby authorize [Name of Practice] to (check those that apply):

__ use the following protected health information, and/or

__ disclose the following protected health information to [Name of entity to receive information]:

_____

_____

[Specifically describe the information to be used or disclosed, including, but not limited to, meaningful descriptors such as date of service, type of service provided, level of detail to be released, origin of information, etc.]

This protected health information is being used or disclosed for the following purposes:

_____

_____

[List specific purposes here.]

This authorization shall be in force and effect until [specify (1) date or (2) event that relates to the patient or the purpose of the use or disclosure] at which time this authorization to use or disclose this protected health information expires.

I understand that I have the right to revoke this authorization, in writing, at any time by sending such written notification to [Name of Privacy Contact] at [office address or e-mail address]. I understand that a revocation is not effective to the extent that [Name of Practice] has relied on the use or disclosure of the protected health information.

▲

HIPAA Authorization Form, continued

I understand that information used or disclosed pursuant to this authorization may be subject to redisclosure by the recipient and may no longer be protected by federal or state law.

[Name of Practice] will not condition my treatment, payment, enrollment in a health plan or eligibility for benefits (if applicable) on whether I provide authorization for the requested use or disclosure.

I understand that I have the right to:

Inspect or copy the protected health information to be used or disclosed as permitted under federal law (or state law to the extent the state law provides greater access rights.)

Refuse to sign this authorization.

[The use or disclosure requested under this authorization will result in direct or indirect remuneration to the [Name of Practice] from a third party.] [If applicable.]

_____
Signature of Patient or Personal Representative

_____
Date

_____
Name of Patient or Personal Representative

_____
Description of Personal Representative's Authority

Form provided courtesy of Medical Association of Billers, www.e-medbill.com

Sample Policy Guidance For HIPAA Security

ABC Health Clinic
123 Main Street
Anywhere, USA 12345

Subject: Guidance for HIPAA Security Policies, Procedures

Purpose

ABC Health Clinic is committed to ensuring the privacy and security of protected health information. Federal, state, and/or local laws and regulations have established standards with which health care organizations must comply to ensure the security and confidentiality of protected health information. To support our commitment to security of patient health information, all employees of ABC Health Clinic will receive appropriate training, as required under 45 CFR 164.308.

Policy

(1) All employees of ABC Health Clinic, to include management aand staff members, shall receive training regarding security awareness.

(2) System Users of ABC Health Clinic shall receive training regarding:

   (a) Protection from malicious software use (including virus protection);

   (b) Periodic security updates;

   (c) Log-in; and

   (d) Password management.

(3) ABC Health Clinic's Security Official/Chief Security Official is responsible for the development and delivery of security training.

(4) ABC Health Clinic's Security Official/Chief Security Official will periodically send out security reminders to make clinic employees, as well as billing agents, business associates, and contractors, if necessary, aware of security concerns and initiatives on an ongoing basis.

(5) Successful completion of initial and periodically recurring training is a prerequisite for system access and a factor of job performance. A secure record will be maintained by [Individual or Role/Human Resources] tracking training requirement fulfillment for each individual.

(6) Security training policies and procedures may be amended from time to time as necessary to comply with all applicable laws and regulations as well as business associate agreements.

Sample Policy Guidance For HIPAA Security, continued

Procedures

(1) Security training will be based on employee's job responsibilities, and be applicable to members' daily tasks.

(2) Include the importance of security responsibility within the employee's job description.

(3) Education and training on security awareness will include, at least, applicable information regarding the following topics:

    (a) Overall discussion of threats and vulnerabilities specific to electronic protected health information;

    (b) Information access control;

    (c) Personnel clearance levels;

    (d) Incident reporting;

    (e) Viruses and other forms of malicious software;

    (f) User log-in;

    (g) Password maintenance;

    (h) Social engineering;

    (i) Security principles;] and

    (j) HIPAA and organizational privacy and security rules, policies and procedures, and the sanctions, and civil and criminal penalties prescribed for wrongful actions.

(4) Information access control education will include, at least:

    (a) Access limitations, including procedures for acquiring additional accesses (or removing accesses) if necessary;

    (b) Controls in place for regulating access to information.

(5) Personnel clearance level education will include, at least:

    (a) Clearance level limitations, including procedures for changing levels if necessary;

    (b) Controls in place for regulating access to information based on clearance levels.

(6) Incident reporting education will include, at least:

    (a) Symptoms of an incident;

    (b) Persons to notify immediately in the event of a suspected incident;

    (c) Emphasis on not disclosing the incident to persons without a need to know;

    (d) Any applicable steps to contain the incident (e.g., disconnect the network cable, but leave the power on).

(7) Virus protection (malicious code) education will include, at least:
   (a) Potential harm that can be caused by viruses;
   (b) Prevention of viruses;
   (c) What to do if a virus is detected.

(8) User log-in education will include, at least:
   (a) Configuration of components to record log-in attempts (both successful and unsuccessful), as well as automated lockout and reporting after [X] failed attempts.
   (b) Importance of monitoring log-in success of failure.
   (c) Steps for checking last log-in information, and reporting suspicious information.
   (d) How to report discrepancies of log-in.
   (e) User's responsibility to ensure the security of health care information.

(9) Password management education will include, at least:
   (a) Rules to be following in creating and changing passwords, including password adequacy (e.g., length, complexity) and frequency considerations; and
   (b) Importance of keeping passwords confidential, to include storage considerations.

(10) Social engineering education will include, at least:
   (a) Emphasis on adhering first to all published policies and procedures, despite claims by persons that they should do otherwise;
   (b) Emphasis on the practice of verifying an official's identity, position and/or authority prior to taking direction from that person with respect to security measures; and
   (c) A sampling of common "social engineering" measures and countermeasures.

(11) Security principle education will include, at least:
   (a) Principle of need to know, least privilege;
   (b) Principle of separation of duties;
   (c) Principle of dual control;
   (d) Principle of least resistance;
   (e) Principle of defense in depth; and
   (f) Processes for suggesting security improvements based on these principles.

(12) Standards, policies and procedures will include, at least:
   (a) HIPAA security standard overview;

▲

Sample Policy Guidance For HIPAA Security, continued

(b) Overview of policies and procedures, including how to access and gain clarification regarding such; and

(c) Discussion of sanctions and other penalties, as well as the potential for violations to be reported to external agencies.

(13) Security training will be delivered to all workforce members during initial orientation, and thereafter at least annually.

(14) Issue periodic reminders and security updates, to include topics on password security, malicious software, incident identification and response, access control, and last log-in monitoring.

(15) Utilize broadcast e-mail for routine reminders every [Period]. Out of cycle/band reminders can be issued for urgent updates, such as new threats, hazards, vulnerabilities and/or countermeasures.

(16) The policies and procedures established herein, including all derivative documents regarding security measures will be documented and maintained in a current manner.

Form provided courtesy of Medical Billers Association of America, www.e-medbill.com

New Medical Biller Proposal/Agreement

Medical Billing Proposal/Agreement

Name of Provider Practice:_____

Address:_____

City, State and Zip Code:_____

Phone_____ Fax:_____ E-Mail:_____

Name of Medical Biller: _____

Address: _____

City, State and Zip Code: _____

Phone_____ Fax:_____ E-Mail:_____

This is a Proposal/Agreement between the provider and Medical Biller named above. The Provider is requesting the following services from Medical Biller:

_____ Contracted Carrier Paper and Electronic Claims Submission

_____ Non-Contracted Carrier Paper and Electronic Claims Submission

_____ Payment Posting

_____ Appeals of Contracted Claims Denials or Adverse Benefit Determinations

_____ Recovery of Accounts Receivables

_____ Patient Billing

_____ Verification of Benefits and Patient Information

The provider is requesting that the Medical Biller provide the above requested services:

_____ In Office

_____ At Home

It is understood between both the Provider and Medical Biller, that the patient information, which includes demographic and insurance information, charges, CPT and ICD-9-CM codes used by the Provider, claims and patient statement information are the property of the Provider and not the property of the Medical Biller. The Medical Biller will make every reasonable attempt to keep this information secure against fire, theft, and any unauthorized disclosures. In the event of termination of this Agreement, Medical Biller will return any and all information to the Provider in a manner requested by the Provider and in a format that the Provider can still use. Failure to do so may subject the Medical Biller to a lawsuit for loss of revenue.

▲

New Medical Biller Proposal/Agreement, continued

The Medical Biller is a Business Associate of the Provider. Any and all information that is given to the Medical Biller must be kept private and confidential. Any unauthorized disclosure is grounds for immediate termination and subject to possible lawsuits.

In order for the Medical Biller to perform his/her job, it is imperative that the information given to the Medical Biller be 100% true, accurate and correct. This information must be verified by the Provider's staff prior to being given to the Medical Biller. The Medical Biller will take this information and use it to submit claims and statements and any additional tasks requested by the Provider. The Provider and Provider's staff fully understands the consequences of submitting a claim with incorrect information which can include denial of the claim, investigations and audits by State and Federal regulatory authorities, possible loss of licensure, fines, and/or incarceration. If the Provider wishes the Medical Biller to verify the information, there will be a fee of $5.00 per patient/insurance verification. If the Provider does not want the Medical Biller to verify the information given to the Medical Biller, then the Provider holds the Medical Biller harmless from any actions that may result from using unverified information.

When submitting paper and electronic claims, the Medical Biller will ensure that the information received from the Provider is entered into the Medical Biller's or Provider's medical billing software program with 100% accuracy based on the information received. The Medical Biller will check to ensure that any edit errors are corrected to ensure that the claim is a clean claim as defined by State law or Health Insurance-Provider Contract. The Medical Biller will ensure that all claims are submitted in a timely manner as defined by State law, and the Health Insurance-Provider Contract. The fee for submitting claims is 15% of the amount recovered, with the exception of Medicaid Claims. The fee for submitting Medicaid claims is $7.00 per claim.

When submitting claims for workers' compensation or auto accident claims, the Provider must ensure that the injury has been reported to the patient's workers' compensation or auto accident insurance company. The Provider will provide the claim number and adjustor to the Medical Biller. The Medical Biller does not send claims to employers unless allowed under State Workers' Compensation laws. A copy of the medical record and W-9 form will accompany the claim.

When there is a Personal Injury patient who has hired an attorney, the Provider must give the Medical Biller guidance as to what and to whom a bill is to be sent. The Provider must understand that when an attorney has been hired, it can take years to resolve the claim. It is best to bill the patient and the patient can pay and be reimbursed from the settlement, if any. It is also suggested that the Provider do not accept liens or letters of protection without reading the small print where it may state that the Provider accept a considerable discount to the services rendered.

The Provider understands that the Medical Biller must be in compliance with the Compliance laws such as the False Claims Act, Stark I and Stark II, the Anti-Kickback statute and others. These laws deal with discounts, professional courtesy, and write offs of co-pays and deductibles. The Provider must provide the Medical Biller with written documentation, directing the Medical Biller to perform a discount, professional courtesy or to write off a co-pay or deductible, knowing full well of the laws regulating these and absolving the Medical Biller from any action taken by the OIG, Office of Civil Rights, or lawsuits from patients and/or insurance companies.

The Provider is aware that when dealing with non-contracted insurance companies, that it is the patient that has the responsibility of submitting their own claims when seeking care from an out of network provider. The Medical Biller can submit claims for non-contracted carrier patients, however, a copy of the signed Assignment of Benefit Form, and Authorization to Submit Claims Form, along with authorization and pre-certification numbers must be provided to the Medical Biller to accompany the claim. The Provider is aware that when submitting a claim for a non-contracted patient, the insurance company has the right to send the payment of the claim, to the patient. The Medical Biller can attempt to collect the benefit payment from the patient but there is no guarantee of success. The fee for resolving non-contracted patient claims issues is $5.00 per letter/statement. The Provider is also aware that any claims denials or adverse benefit determinations must be resolved by the patient as per their contract with their insurance company. The Provider can only resolve these issues upon receipt of written permission from the patient. The fee for attempting to resolve non-contracted insurance claims issues and adverse benefit determinations is $10 per appeal. In order for the Medical Biller to appeal is for the Provider to give the Medical Biller a copy of the written permission from the patient as well as a copy of the patient's benefit manual which lists the benefits in question as well as the carrier's appeals processes which must be followed to the letter as per Federal Law 29 CFR 2560-503-1.

▲

New Medical Biller Proposal/Agreement, continued

The Provider will give the Medical Biller, a copy of each health insurance contract that the Provider has with each health insurance company. It is important for the Medical Biller to know these contracts as it pertains to the claims submission time-frames, the reimbursement of claims, the time limits for payment of claims, the appeals process and more. The Medical Biller will inform the Provider of any contract violations by the contracted carrier.

In order to establish the Provider into the Medical Biller's software program and to accompany any documents to the various health insurance companies, the Provider will give legible copies of the following documents to Medical Biller:

(1) Medical License
(2) DEA Certificate
(3) Medical School Diploma
(4) Internship Certificate
(5) Residency Certificate
(6) W-9 Form
(7) Medicare Provider Number
(8) Medicaid Provider Number
(9) Tricare Provider Number
(10) Health Insurance Company Provider Number
(11) UPIN
(12) NPI

The Provider will give to the Medical Biller legible copies of the following:
(1) Completed Medical Record and Superbill
(2) Payment Remittances
(3) Health Insurance EOBs
(4) Health Insurance Correspondence
(5) Letters and Subpoenas from Attorneys

When responding to calls, letters and subpoena's for medical information or patient financial information, it can take considerable time and research to provide an attorney with that information. As such, the Medical Biller will charge the attorney, a fee of $25 for each financial statement requested. If a copy of the medical record is requested, this will be sent to the Provider because the Provider is the legal medical records custodian. The patient financial statement will not be released until the Medical Biller receives a HIPAA Authorization for Release of Information form, signed by the patient.

New Medical Biller Proposal/Agreement, continued

Sending statements to patients can be very costly, especially if the patient provided incorrect addresses, phone numbers, and does not respond to statements. This is why the Provider may want to consider collecting co-pays and deductibles at the time of service. This reduces administrative costs and increases revenue for the practice. If the Provider wishes the Medical Biller to send statements to patients, the Provider agrees that the Medical Biller is not responsible for the patient information received from the Provider. The Medical Biller will send a total of three statements. The fee for each statement is $5.00. If the patient has not responded to the three statements, the Provider must decide what to do with the account. If the Provider wishes the account be sent to the Provider's debt collection agency, the Medical Biller will send the account to the debt collection agency. Once the account is in the hands of the debt collection agency, the Medical Biller is absolved of any responsibility for the account. If the debt collection agency obtains verified health insurance information and the Provider requests that the Medical Biller submit the claim, the fee for submitting the claim is $10.00 per claim. Upon submitting the claim, the account will be closed by the Medical Biller. The Provider will report any payments received to the debt collection agency.

Working accounts receivables entails performing extensive research on claims that are older than 90 days from the date of service. The Medical Biller will work accounts receivables that are older than 90 days from the date of service. The Medical Biller may find that payment was already sent to the provider but not reported to the Medical Biller. If this does happen, there is a $5.00 fee per account for researching the account that was previously paid. If the patient received the payment, then the patient will have to be billed. The fee for billing patient is listed above. The fee for working accounts receivables is 15% of the amount recovered.

Appealing a denied claim or an incorrectly paid claim, for those carriers that are contracted with the Provider, can be very extensive and time consuming. Examples of denials are:
(1) Timely Filing
(2) Inclusive
(3) Medically Necessary
(4) Payment less than the contracted amount
(5) Retroactive Denials

The Medical Biller can appeal these types of issues. The fee for doing so is 15% of the amount recovered.

▲

New Medical Biller Proposal/Agreement, continued

There may be times when an overpayment has been made by a patient or insurance company. If the Medical Biller identifies an overpayment, the Provider will be informed and given copies of the documents to show the overpayment. The Provider is responsible for issuing the refund to the patient and/or insurance company. A copy of the refund payment will be given to the Medical Biller for entry into the patient's account.

The Provider and Medical Biller will meet on a weekly basis to go over claims issues and other subjects as desired by either the Medical Biller or the Provider.

The Provider is responsible for resolving any "bad checks" received from a patient or insurance company. A copy of the bad check will be given to the Medical Biller for entry into the patient's account. If the check was resolved, the Medical Biller will be provided with this information.

The Medical Biller will provide the Provider with "End of Month" reports such as:
(1) Aging Report
(2) Charges/Payments/Adjustment Report
(3) Accounts to Debt Collections
(4) Any other reports as needed.

In the event of the termination of this agreement, it is agreed that either party has the right to terminate this agreement, without cause. It is best that before terminating the agreement, both parties attempt to meet and work out any issues that led to discussing termination. If the final decision is to terminate, either party will give the other party a written notice of termination, at least ninety (90) days before the termination date. Both parties understand that even though a letter of termination and a termination date has been given, the Medical Biller will be sending claims up to the date of termination. These claims must still be resolved, and payments have to be posted. Patients will still be sending payments that have to be posted, so to fully stop is impossible and it can cause financial ruin for the provider. In Medical Billing, the termination date will be the last date of service that claims will be sent. If a new medical billing company has been hired, the new medical billing company will begin sending claims with a new date of service. Payments will be coming in that the Provider must sort and distribute. These payments will be based on the date of service. If the Provider wishes the new medical billing company to resolve the claims from the previous Medical Biller, then the Provider must understand that the previous Medical Biller is entitled to receive payment on those claims that are based on a percentage of the amount recovered and the new medical billing company will also want to be reimbursed for posting payments, sending claims, appealing denials, etc. Therefore, there must be a settlement offer to the previous Medical Biller on those claims if the Provider wants to cut off the previous Medical Biller completely, otherwise, the previous Medical Biller will work on the closure of the accounts that were worked.

For example. Medical Biller A has been terminated. The termination date is December 31, 2006. Medical Biller B has been hired to work new accounts as of January 1, 2007. Medical Biller A sends claims up to date of service of December 31, 2006. Medical Biller B sends claims as of January 1, 2007. On January 2, 2007, the Provider receives $10,000 in payments on dates of service prior to January 1, 2007. These payments are sent to Medical Biller A to post in the accounts in Medical Biller A's possession. On February 1, 2007, $5,000 in payments are received on dates of service prior to January 1 and $10,000 in payments are received on dates of service after January 1. The $5,000 in payments are sent to Medical Biller A and $10,000 in payments are sent to Medical Biller B. The Provider must review the EOBs and remittances because some will have both dates of service listed. The EOB may show a date of service of November 15, 2006 and a date of service of January 15, 2007. The Medical Billers will be given a copy of the EOB and post appropriately.

The termination letter should give the terminated Medical Biller approximately one year to resolve all claims issues. This ensures quantinuity on receiving payments on a regular basis. At first, there will be monies coming in from both medical billers. As time progresses, less money will be coming in from the terminated medical biller. At the end of the one year time limit, all claims issues should be resolved or the amount to be resolved is so minimal it is no longer an issue. By this time, all patients will be billed, all appeals will be completed and patient responsibility accounts will be at the debt collection agency. The terminated Medical Biller will return any and all documents, and all accounts in the Medical Biller's medical billing software program. This information must be returned to the Provider due to the terminated Medical Biller's authorization to access personal health information being expired. The terminated Medical Biller will no longer be legally allowed access to this information. The information being returned must be in a format that the provider can use such as an an ASCII, Comma, Deliminated form or in Microsoft Database or Spreadsheet. Failure to do this could result in the Medical Biller being sued by the Provider.

New Medical Biller Proposal/Agreement, continued

This Proposal/Agreement is acceptable to both the Provider and Medical Biller. The effective date of this Agreement is _____ 20___.

_____   _____
Signature of Provider   Signature of Medical Biller

_____   _____
Printed Name   Printed Name

_____   _____
Date Date

Copyright (c) 2006, Steven M. Verno, CMBSI
Provided courtesy of Medical Association of Billers, www.e-medbill.com

CMS-1500 Form

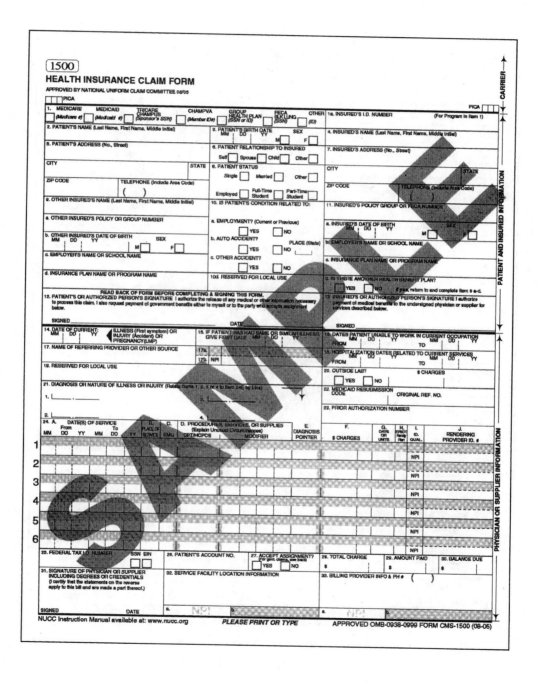

CMS-1500 Form, continued

BECAUSE THIS FORM IS USED BY VARIOUS GOVERNMENT AND PRIVATE HEALTH PROGRAMS, SEE SEPARATE INSTRUCTIONS ISSUED BY APPLICABLE PROGRAMS.

NOTICE: Any person who knowingly files a statement of claim containing any misrepresentation or any false, incomplete or misleading information may be guilty of a criminal act punishable under law and may be subject to civil penalties.

REFERS TO GOVERNMENT PROGRAMS ONLY

MEDICARE AND CHAMPUS PAYMENTS: A patient's signature requests that payment be made and authorizes release of any information necessary to process the claim and certifies that the information provided in Blocks 1 through 12 is true, accurate and complete. In the case of a Medicare claim, the patient's signature authorizes any entity to release to Medicare medical and nonmedical information, including employment status, and whether the person has employer group health insurance, liability, no-fault, worker's compensation or other insurance which is responsible to pay for the services for which the Medicare claim is made. See 42 CFR 411.24(a). If item 9 is completed, the patient's signature authorizes release of the information to the health plan or agency shown. In Medicare assigned or CHAMPUS participation cases, the physician agrees to accept the charge determination of the Medicare carrier or CHAMPUS fiscal intermediary as the full charge, and the patient is responsible only for the deductible, coinsurance and noncovered services. Coinsurance and the deductible are based upon the charge determination of the Medicare carrier or CHAMPUS fiscal intermediary if this is less than the charge submitted. CHAMPUS is not a health insurance program but makes payment for health benefits provided through certain affiliations with the Uniformed Services. Information on the patient's sponsor should be provided in those items captioned in "Insured"; i.e., items 1a, 4, 6, 7, 9, and 11.

BLACK LUNG AND FECA CLAIMS

The provider agrees to accept the amount paid by the Government as payment in full. See Black Lung and FECA instructions regarding required procedure and diagnosis coding systems.

SIGNATURE OF PHYSICIAN OR SUPPLIER (MEDICARE, CHAMPUS, FECA AND BLACK LUNG)

I certify that the services shown on this form were medically indicated and necessary for the health of the patient and were personally furnished by me or were furnished incident to my professional service by my employee under my immediate personal supervision, except as otherwise expressly permitted by Medicare or CHAMPUS regulations.

For services to be considered as "incident" to a physician's professional service, 1) they must be rendered under the physician's immediate personal supervision by his/her employee, 2) they must be an integral, although incidental part of a covered physician's service, 3) they must be of kinds commonly furnished in physician's offices, and 4) the services of nonphysicians must be included on the physician's bills.

For CHAMPUS claims, I further certify that I (or any employee) who rendered services am not an active duty member of the Uniformed Services or a civilian employee of the United States Government or a contract employee of the United States Government, either civilian or military (refer to 5 USC 5536). For Black-Lung claims, I further certify that the services performed were for a Black Lung-related disorder.

No Part B Medicare benefits may be paid unless this form is received as required by existing law and regulations (42 CFR 424.32).

NOTICE: Any one who misrepresents or falsifies essential information to receive payment from Federal funds requested by this form may upon conviction be subject to fine and imprisonment under applicable Federal laws.

NOTICE TO PATIENT ABOUT THE COLLECTION AND USE OF MEDICARE, CHAMPUS, FECA, AND BLACK LUNG INFORMATION
(PRIVACY ACT STATEMENT)

We are authorized by CMS, CHAMPUS and OWCP to ask you for information needed in the administration of the Medicare, CHAMPUS, FECA, and Black Lung programs. Authority to collect information is in section 205(a), 1862, 1872 and 1874 of the Social Security Act as amended, 42 CFR 411.24(a) and 424.5(a) (6), and 44 USC 3101;41 CFR 101 et seq and 10 USC 1079 and 1086; 5 USC 8101 et seq; and 30 USC 901 et seq; 38 USC 613; E.O. 9397.

The information we obtain to complete claims under these programs is used to identify you and to determine your eligibility. It is also used to decide if the services and supplies you received are covered by these programs and to insure that proper payment is made.

The information may also be given to other providers of services, carriers, intermediaries, medical review boards, health plans, and other organizations or Federal agencies, for the effective administration of Federal provisions that require other third parties payers to pay primary to Federal program, and as otherwise necessary to administer these programs. For example, it may be necessary to disclose information about the benefits you have used to a hospital or doctor. Additional disclosures are made through routine uses for information contained in systems of records.

FOR MEDICARE CLAIMS: See the notice modifying system No. 09-70-0501, titled, 'Carrier Medicare Claims Record,' published in the Federal Register, Vol. 55 No. 177, page 37549, Wed. Sept. 12, 1990, or as updated and republished.

FOR OWCP CLAIMS: Department of Labor, Privacy Act of 1974, "Republication of Notice of Systems of Records," Federal Register Vol. 55 No. 40, Wed Feb. 28, 1990, See ESA-5, ESA-6, ESA-12, ESA-13, ESA-30, or as updated and republished.

FOR CHAMPUS CLAIMS: PRINCIPLE PURPOSE(S): To evaluate eligibility for medical care provided by civilian sources and to issue payment upon establishment of eligibility and determination that the services/supplies received are authorized by law.

ROUTINE USE(S): Information from claims and related documents may be given to the Dept. of Veterans Affairs, the Dept. of Health and Human Services and/or the Dept. of Transportation consistent with their statutory administrative responsibilities under CHAMPUS/CHAMPVA; to the Dept. of Justice for representation of the Secretary of Defense in civil actions; to the Internal Revenue Service, private collection agencies, and consumer reporting agencies in connection with recoupment claims; and to Congressional Offices in response to inquiries made at the request of the person to whom a record pertains. Appropriate disclosures may be made to other federal, state, local, foreign government agencies, private business entities, and individual providers of care, on matters relating to entitlement, claims adjudication, fraud, program abuse, utilization review, quality assurance, peer review, program integrity, third-party liability, coordination of benefits, and civil and criminal litigation related to the operation of CHAMPUS.

DISCLOSURES: Voluntary; however, failure to provide information will result in delay in payment or may result in denial of claim. With the one exception discussed below, there are no penalties under these programs for refusing to supply information. However, failure to furnish information regarding the medical services rendered or the amount charged would prevent payment of claims under these programs. Failure to furnish any other information, such as name or claim number, would delay payment of the claim. Failure to provide medical information under FECA could be deemed an obstruction.

It is mandatory that you tell us if you know that another party is responsible for paying for your treatment. Section 1128B of the Social Security Act and 31 USC 3801-3812 provide penalties for withholding this information.

You should be aware that P.L. 100-503, the "Computer Matching and Privacy Protection Act of 1988", permits the government to verify information by way of computer matches.

MEDICAID PAYMENTS (PROVIDER CERTIFICATION)

I hereby agree to keep such records as are necessary to disclose fully the extent of services provided to individuals under the State's Title XIX plan and to furnish information regarding any payments claimed for providing such services as the State Agency or Dept. of Health and Human Services may request.

I further agree to accept, as payment in full, the amount paid by the Medicaid program for those claims submitted for payment under that program, with the exception of authorized deductible, coinsurance, co-payment or similar cost-sharing charge.

SIGNATURE OF PHYSICIAN (OR SUPPLIER): I certify that the services listed above were medically indicated and necessary to the health of this patient and were personally furnished by me or my employee under my personal direction.

NOTICE: This is to certify that the foregoing information is true, accurate and complete. I understand that payment and satisfaction of this claim will be from Federal and State funds, and that any false claims, statements, or documents, or concealment of a material fact, may be prosecuted under applicable Federal or State laws.

According to the Paperwork Reduction Act of 1995, no persons are required to respond to a collection of information unless it displays a valid OMB control number. The valid OMB control number for this information collection is 0938-0999. The time required to complete this information collection is estimated to average 10 minutes per response, including the time to review instructions, search existing data resources, gather the data needed, and complete and review the information collection. If you have any comments concerning the accuracy of the time estimate(s) or suggestions for improving this form, please write to: CMS, Attn: PRA Reports Clearance Officer, 7500 Security Boulevard, Baltimore, Maryland 21244-1850. This address is for comments and/or suggestions only. DO NOT MAIL COMPLETED CLAIM FORMS TO THIS ADDRESS.

Form provided courtesy of the National Uniform Claim Committee, www.nucc.org

Glossary

Accept assignment: term meaning the provider accepts Medicare's approved fee for his services.

Administrator: the insurance company that writes and administers the insurance policy; also known as the insurer, underwriter, or carrier.

Allowable: the portion, usually 70 percent to 80 percent, paid by the insurer for covered services.

Annual maximum: maximum amount a policy will pay in a benefit year or calendar year, depending on the terms of the policy.

Antigen: substance that induces the formation of antibodies.

ASO: administrative services only; see third-party administrator.

▲

Audit/Error report: report generated by the clearinghouse to notify biller of rejected claims; also called a sender log.

Basic plan: commercial plan that pays total costs up to a stated maximum for all but a few exclusions; costs may be incurred in the hospital, at the doctor's office, or at home; may or may not feature deductible.

Beneficiary: the person eligible to receive benefits under the insurance policy; the patient.

Benefits verification: see predetermination.

Birthday rule: in cases of multiple dependent insurance coverage, the determination of primary coverage by parents' birth dates.

Carrier: the insurance company that writes and administers the insurance policy; also known as the insurer, underwriter, or administrator.

CDT: common name for Dental Terminology; system of coding dental and orthodontic procedures. Updated on an annual basis.

Certificate holder: see Insured.

CHAMPUS: Civilian Health and Medical Program for the Uniformed Services; provides dependents of active and retired military personnel and their families with civilian health-care coverage.

Charge slip: see Superbill.

Clean claim: one that does not need correction.

Clearinghouse: a company that receives and transmits claims electronically.

CMS: The Centers for Medicare and Medicaid Services. Previously known as the Health Care Financing Administration (HCFA).

CMS 1500: form on which all medical insurance claims must be sent, formerly known as the HCFA 1500.

Co-insurance: the percent the patient pays for covered services as opposed to the amount the carrier pays.

Comprehensive plan: commercial plan; composite of both basic and major medical coverage.

Coordination of benefits: insurance policy provision stating that when a patient is covered by more than one group plan, the total benefits paid by all policies are limited to 100 percent of the charges.

Co-payment: the balance of payment for covered services paid by the patient after the insurer pays its portion.

Cost contract: contract between an HMO and Medicare specifying that the HMO's Medicare patients receive all care from that particular HMO.

Cost plan: a point-of-service type of managed care plan in which a patient is allowed to go to outside providers and Medicare will pay its share of the cost.

Coverage verification: see predetermination.

CPT: Current Procedural Terminology; refers to a system of coding services, procedures, and supplies developed by the American Medical Association.

Cross-over contract: a type of Medigap contract in which Medicare automatically forwards claims to the Medigap carrier.

Cross-over patient: one who has Medicare as his primary coverage and Medicaid as a supplemental.

Current Procedural Terminology: see CPT.

Customary fee: fee basis determined by insurers based on 90 percent of fees charged by all doctors in the same specialty in the same geographic area.

Day sheet: page used by provider to list all daily superbill information on a single sheet rather than send one superbill per patient to the outsource biller.

Deductible: the amount the patient must pay before the insurance coverage begins to kick in.

Dependent: spouse, child, or other person for whom the insured is legally responsible.

Drop claim to paper: a service in which a clearinghouse prints and mails a paper version of a claim received online.

Dual coverage: a term meaning a patient is covered by two or more insurance policies.

Durable medical equipment: walkers, wheelchairs, hospital beds, and other equipment used in and around the home because of medical necessity.

EDI: Electronic Data Interchange; sends information electronically from one computer to another.

Elective procedure: a medical procedure not requiring immediate action.

Electronic Data Interchange: see EDI.

E/M: evaluation and management; the portion of the CPT codes used to categorize physician visits.

Enrollee: see Insured.

EOB: explanation of benefits; the carrier uses this to summarize the details of a submitted claim and its reimbursement.

EPO: exclusive provider organization; a type of managed care organization.

Epoetin: used in the treatment of home dialysis patients.

ESRD: end-stage renal disease, a kidney malfunction.

Evaluation and management: see E/M.

Exclusions: services or problems not covered by the insurance carrier.

Exclusive provider organization: see EPO.

Explanation of benefits: see EOB.

Fee-for-service plan: commercial plan in which subscribers make monthly payments that entitle them to coverage.

Full-practice management: the practice of handling all aspects of a doctor's accounting as opposed to strictly processing claims.

GP: general practitioner.

Gross income: the amount of income before expenses are deducted.

Group policy: commercial policy written for and purchased by groups or employers for their members or employees.

HCFA: the Health Care Financing Administration, which is now known as the Centers for Medicare and Medicaid Services (CMS). See CMS.

HCFA Common Procedure Coding System: see HCPCS.

HCFA 1500: form on which all medical insurance claims must be sent, which has been updated and is now called the CMS 1500.

HCPCS: HCFA Common Procedure Coding System; the CPT coding system devised by the American Medical Association.

Health Maintenance Organization: see HMO.

HIPAA: the Health Insurance Portability and Accountability Act of 1996, which is designed to protect patient privacy by protecting personal health information.

HMO: Health Maintenance Organization; a managed care type of provider service in which patients pay a monthly fee to belong.

ICD-10: international classification of diseases; a system of coding diseases developed by the World Health Organization; also called ICD-10-CM for Clinical Modification.

Indemnify: to reimburse health expenses.

Indemnity policy: a policy in which the carrier reimburses the patient for covered services up to a limit set in the policy.

Independent Practice Association: see IPA.

Individual/Family deductible: under some policies, each covered family member must meet a deductible; under other policies, all of the family's medical expenses go toward meeting one deductible.

Individual policy: commercial policy written for and purchased by an individual or an individual and his family as opposed to a group policy.

Insured: the policy holder; the person covered by the policy, who, because he's covered (as in a group policy), makes it possible for his family to be covered; also known as the enrollee, certificate holder, or subscriber.

Insurer: the insurance company that writes and administers the insurance policy; also known as the carrier, underwriter, or administrator.

Intermediaries: commercial carriers that handle Medicare claims.

IPA: Independent Practice Association; a type of managed care organization.

Level II: branch of the HCPCS coding system relating to durable medical equipment, medical supplies, and chemotherapy, among other miscellaneous services.

Level III: HCPCS codes used on a local level by Medicare.

Lifetime maximum: the total amount the policy will pay for a certain condition or problem.

Limiting charge: the amount providers who do not accept assignment can charge over and above the Medicare-approved amount.

Listed exclusions: specific services, procedures, or supplies not covered by the policy and therefore not paid for owners, but can be useful if you want some added protection for your personal assets.

Lock-in requirements: see Cost contract.

Major medical plan: commercial plan designed for catastrophic situations such as extended hospitalization; does not pay for minor health problems or office visits and usually features large deductible and co-payments.

Managed Service Organization: see MSO.

Maximums: the top or maximum amounts a policy will pay.

Medicaid: insurance program administered by CMS and each state's government for people at or near poverty level.

Medicare: insurance coverage for those over age 65, younger people suffering from end-stage renal disease, and those who have been collecting Social Security disability benefits for more than two years.

Medigap: supplemental Medicare coverage.

Minimum Premium Plan: group self-insured program in which the employer provides funds for claims up to a certain dollar amount and then pays a commercial carrier to take on the remaining risk.

MPP: see Minimum Premium Plan.

MSO: Managed Service Organization; a type of managed care organization.

Neurology: medical specialty dealing with the nervous system and its diseases.

Nonduplication of benefits: see coordination of benefits.

Non-PAR: a provider who declines to accept Medicare assignment.

Oncology: medical specialty concerned with tumors.

Outsource billing service: one that performs its work outside the provider's office.

PAR: see Participating physician.

Part A Medicare: covers inpatient hospitalization, skilled nursing, and hospice and home health-care services.

Part B Medicare: covers doctors' services, outpatient hospital care, X-rays, lab tests, ambulance services, durable medical equipment, and other nonhospitalization services.

Participating physician: a provider who accepts Medicare assignment; also called a PAR.

Pneumococcal: organism responsible for infections including pneumonia, bronchitis, and meningitis.

Podiatrist: foot disorder specialist.

Point-of-service plan: see Cost plan.

POS: point-of-service managed care plan; see Cost plan.

PPO: Preferred Provider Organization; a managed care organization in which a group of doctors cooperates with an insurance plan by accepting fee-for-service payments at less than the usual and customary rate.

Precertification: term used when the insurance carrier requires the provider to receive permission before performing a service.

Predetermination: term used when the doctor determines the maximum amount he will pay for certain services, procedures, and supplies before performing or providing them; also called coverage or benefits verification.

Pre-existing condition: a disease, medical condition, or problem the patient already has before he applies for insurance or before the policy takes effect.

Preferred Provider Organization: see PPO.

Primary physician: in an HMO-type plan, this is the patient's preassigned physician.

Provider: anyone who provides health-care services and/or supplies, e.g., ambulance service, biofeedback technician, dentist, durable equipment purveyor, pharmacist, or social worker, in addition to all types of medical doctors.

Psychoneurotic: refers to a type of mental illness that is not as severe as a psychosis or character disorder; neurosis.

RBRVS: Resource-Based Relative Value Scale arrives at a reasonable charge based on: a) the actual amount of work performed by the doctor; b) the doctor's expenses, excluding malpractice insurance; and c) the cost of malpractice insurance.

Reasonable fee: fee rate determined by insurers based on the least of: a) the fee the doctor has billed, b) the usual fee, c) the customary fee, or d) another specially justifiable fee.

Reassignment: to assign payment to a third party.

Resource-Based Relative Value Scale: see RBRVS.

Secondary claim: one in which two members of a family are supplementally covered by each other's insurance policies.

Self-insured plan: type of group insurance in which the employer rather than an insurance company provides the funds to pay its employees' claims.

Sender log: see audit/error report.

Stop-loss provision: limits the total co-payments the beneficiary must pay in a given year.

Subscriber: see insured.

Superbill: also called a charge slip; lists the services and procedures commonly performed by the provider and gives the patient's name, date of visit, and any charges.

Third-party administrator: an insurance or specialized management company that administers a group self-insured plan.

TPA: see third-party administrator.

UB92: form used to bill Part A Medicare.

UCR: see Usual, customary, and reasonable.

Underwriter: the insurance company that writes and administers the insurance policy; also known as the insurer, carrier, or administrator.

Urologist: physician specializing in diseases of the urinary tract in both sexes and of the genital tract in the male.

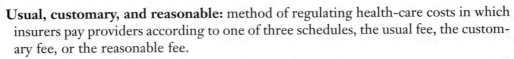

Usual, customary, and reasonable: method of regulating health-care costs in which insurers pay providers according to one of three schedules, the usual fee, the customary fee, or the reasonable fee.

Usual fee: the usual or normal amount doctors charge for a specific service as determined by insurers who keep annual tabs and then compute an average fee.

WHO: World Health Organization.

Workers' compensation: provides private insurance coverage for workers who become ill or injured while on the job.

Index